Praise for *It's About Time!*

I love this book! *It's About Time!* is exactly what disorganized procrastinators like me want and need: a calm, clear-headed, and organized person to help us fix our messy lives and minds. In a calm, kind, reassuring, and nonjudgmental voice, Mitzi shows us how small simple tweaks to daily habits can lead to huge positive change.

Laura Zigman
Wife, mother, novelist, ghostwriter,
paper-hoarder, and slob

In today's hurried life, it's hard to find time to have fun, be with the people you love, and of course, make time to simply sit back and relax. Sound familiar? Well, if you think *It's About Time!* to change all that, then you'll find this A–Z book a fabulous guide to help streamline your work and home so you can enjoy more time doing the things you love. This is a step-by-step guide for organizing and streamlining your daily processes as well as delegating tasks. Each chapter tackles one chaos at a time and helps you to find order again. This way, little by little, you'll craft a more balanced, productive, and enjoyable life.

Dr. Rosina McAlpine
Associate professor, the University of Sydney Business School
Founding director, Inspired Children
www.DrRosina.com

D0877984

It's About Time! gives you a fresh start on what matters most. Mitzi Weinman ingeniously furnishes real people with new skills to make time for their highest priorities. Her approach is personal and motivating.

X marks a treasure, and Mitzi Weinman provides that and more with *It's About Time!* Whether managing a corporation or teaching children foundational life skills, her tips for success in life's mandatory curriculum are guaranteed to exponentially enhance productivity and sanity.

It's About Time!

Transforming Chaos into Calm, A to Z

MITZI WEINMAN

iUniverse LLC
Bloomington

IT'S ABOUT TIME!
TRANSFORMING CHAOS INTO CALM, A TO Z

iUniverse books may be ordered through booksellers or by contacting:

iUniverse
1663 Liberty Drive
Bloomington, IN 47403
www.iuniverse.com
1-800-Authors (1-800-288-4677)

Because of the dynamic nature of the Internet, any web addresses or links contained in this book may have changed since publication and may no longer be valid. The views expressed in this work are solely those of the author and do not necessarily reflect the views of the publisher, and the publisher hereby disclaims any responsibility for them.

Any people depicted in stock imagery provided by Thinkstock are models, and such images are being used for illustrative purposes only. Certain stock imagery © Thinkstock.

ISBN: 978-1-4917-3262-5 (sc)
ISBN: 978-1-4917-3405-6 (e)

Library of Congress Control Number: 2014908120

Printed in the United States of America.

iUniverse rev. date: 06/13/14

To my *rocks*, Stu and Jonathan.
To those who find joy dancing through
life and are willing to defy gravity.

Contents

Preface

I have had so many people say to me that I must have been *born* organized. Every time I hear that, I have to laugh, because when I was growing up, my father put a sign on my bedroom door that read:

> *Cleanliness is next to godliness;*
> *welcome to the gates of hell.*

I didn't have "a place for everything," except the floor. I was quite a slob, or so I was told. Maybe I was lazy.

When I was seven, I ran away from home because I didn't want to make my bed. I decided to leave home with my baby carriage and clothes in tow. I walked four miles across town to my babysitter's house. Neighbors, friends, and police were scouring the area looking for a small, curly-headed girl who didn't want to make her bed. To this day, I don't like making my bed, and I am ever grateful for having a comforter. *Whoosh*, and my bed is made.

Having a messy and disorganized bedroom was one thing, but the problem extended beyond the gates of hell into the land of *procrastination*. I always waited until the last minute to do my homework.

I was a good student, but I had difficulty reading and struggled with comprehension. I didn't know how to approach homework, break my assignments down into small bite-size doable pieces, and plan how I would get my schoolwork done.

I hadn't learned these life skills by observation, as some young people do. And no one explicitly taught me. So I didn't realize their importance. My philosophy was that the longer I could postpone doing my work, the better. I was wrong.

Merlin Olsen, the football player, sports commentator, and actor, said it best: "One of life's most painful moments comes when we must admit that we didn't do our homework, that we are not prepared." I struggled and had many painful moments.

When I went off to college, suddenly, I had a fresh, clean start. I didn't have a lot of *stuff*. I organized my dorm room and rethought my approach to schoolwork. For the first time, I felt organized, and it felt good!

When I started TimeFinder in 1989, my vision was, and still is, to give my clients a fresh, clean start, just as I had when I went to college. I want them to feel the pleasure and relief that I felt in being organized and getting things done in a less stressful way.

During TimeFinder's early years, I, like so many of us, faced a difficult time in my life. My mother had complications from a minor car accident that lead to a subdural hematoma and, subsequently, a severe brain bleed. At the same time, my boyfriend, Stu (who later became my husband), had his own tragedy. Stu's dad was having a bone-marrow transplant at the Fred Hutchinson Cancer Research Center in Seattle. While my mom was in the ICU at Brigham & Women's Hospital in Boston, Stu had to fly to Seattle to be with his dad and family because of complications from the transplant.

A few days after Stu arrived in Seattle, his father passed away. My mom remained in hospitals, rehabs, and skilled nursing facilities for the next two and a half years before she passed away.

I learned an awful lot during this time. I learned, as difficult as it was, that I needed to remain focused on my business while dealing with insurance, legal issues, and house matters for my mom and dad. I learned to be an advocate for my mom who, literally, didn't have a voice.

I developed a stronger compassion for those who are facing life's obstacles and are distracted during difficult times in their lives, but I wouldn't let anyone pity me during that time, and I remain adamant that pity parties don't help anyone—actions do!

As you read this book, written so that each chapter is independent of any other chapter, my hope is that you will be able to—no matter what you are doing in your life or where you are on your magnificent journey—learn the life skills of organization and planning so that you will not know, as I did, the pain of being unprepared. My hope is that *It's About Time!* will make it easier for you to take one step at a time in the process of "*Transforming Chaos into Calm, A to Z.*"

Acknowledgments

There are many people I wish to thank for their support, encouragement, and honesty as I journeyed out to write this book, which was many years in the making, with lots of starts and stops. I am grateful to be able to acknowledge those who have stood by me:

My son Jonathan, who always shares words of encouragement, gives me big hugs, and says, "You're doing good, Mommy."

My husband, Stu Perlmutter, the most honest man I know.

My parents, Julia and Ralph Weinman. Even though they aren't here to share in this accomplishment, they were always supportive and proud of the work I was doing.

Janet Bosworth, editor extraordinaire for *It's About Time!*

Robin Zucker, Kas Zucker Design, www.kaszuckerdesign. com, for her wonderful illustrations.

Carol MacGregor, photographer, Happy Gatherings, www. HappyGatherings.com.

Thank you to Judith Bowman, Dr. Lawrence J. Epstein, Gina Ghioldi, Deborah King, Patty LePrie, Ned Mahoney, Mia Melanson, JoAnne Powers, Joan Sawler, Randi Siegal, Yvonne Sum, my family, friends, and clients.

Introduction

My objective in writing this book is to help busy people with their time, keeping in mind that they may not have the time to read it—what an interesting paradox! The reality is that people with differing lifestyles and work styles face similar time challenges as they rush around feeling overwhelmed by undone tasks. The ultimate goal of this book is show you that taking action will make you successful in gaining more control in common everyday circumstances.

The myth of "time management" is that time can actually be managed. This myth has been espoused for years and must be debunked. Managing time is an effort that goes unrewarded; putting a great deal of energy in this area is overrated at best and, ultimately, futile. We need to shift from managing our time to managing ourselves. How do your habits work against you? Can new habits make changes for the better? Do you have the desire and commitment to change your current modus operandi?

Think about how you react to situations. Your reaction will either keep you in control of your day or have you spinning and reeling, making it difficult to get back on track. You already know what's working and what's not. This book will help you reassess your current approach to work or home situations and find doable solutions that *will* work.

The emphasis of *It's About Time!* is on taking action to move toward your desired results. As you do this, you will notice a positive impact on your productivity and time effectiveness each and every day.

A few letters have bonus chapters. When there was a letter that had a second concept that I thought was important to share or felt remiss about omitting, I added a bonus chapter. For example, the book begins with "A: Action," followed by a bonus *A* chapter, "Anticipation."

Throughout *It's About Time!* the use of the task list, planner or calendar is recommended. These tools can be paper or electronic.

Each chapter ends with a number of "next steps." These should help to make this process a bit easier. Though I'd like to tell you it's a simple process, it isn't, at least once you move beyond minor adjustments to your current habits and practices. It is a process, and it never ends. I am still working on ways to make improvements in my life. Each tweak will be your own, most likely different from anyone else's—and that is okay!

For added help, you will find intentional redundancy throughout *It's About Time!* Many of the ideas overlap other categories in various contexts. The deliberate repetition of ideas is to help reinforce what works.

Repetition + Reinforcement = Remembering + Results

A

Action

**Action: the doing of something; state
of being in motion or of working**

*Being busy does not always mean real work. The object of all
work is production or accomplishment and to either of these
ends there must be forethought, system, planning, intelligence,
and honest purpose, as well as perspiration. Seeming to do
is not doing.—Thomas A. Edison, American inventor*

Ｈow significant to begin *It's About Time! Transforming Chaos into Calm, A to Z* with an *A* for *Action!* You don't need me or a book to tell you that if you want to transform chaos into calm, you need to take action.

Without action, nothing happens, and nothing gets done. *It's About Time!* is about getting where you want to be, one action at a time. Mark Twain said, "There are basically two types of people. People who accomplish things, and people who claim to have accomplished things. The first group is less crowded."

Thinking about what you are going to do is a start, but it won't get you much closer to getting something done. Many people are stymied by their inability to figure out what the first step or next step may be. What derails the process is not taking the time to figure it out and just feeling stuck. The problem with not taking the time to figure out your next step is that you could be taking unnecessary steps or missing instrumental steps that will help you maintain your stride as you move forward.

I was working with a manager who was about to start having more formalized team meetings with his direct reports. He determined the time and day for the initial meeting and entered it into his schedule. I asked him what he needed to do before the meeting. He said that he needed to create an agenda. I asked, "What else?" He looked at me inquisitively and asked what I meant. I asked again, "What steps do you need to take before you can have this meeting?"

Throughout this book, the conclusion of each section is called "Next Steps." The reason for this is that you must determine your very next step or you will stop. What you hoped to do will become an incomplete to-do on your list. Sometimes the next step is determining that you need more information, so you figure out how to get it or who to contact.

Action means getting out of neutral and moving forward. You may need to wash your car, clean a closet, work on a project, or find a new job. Each requires action.

Next Steps

1. Determine what you want to do.
2. Ask yourself, "What do I need to do before I take this action?"
3. Ask again, "What step or piece of information am I missing in order to act?"
4. Once you've identified what the "next steps" are, start doing them.

Bonus A

Anticipate

**Anticipate: to prevent by action in advance;
to be ahead of in doing or achieving**

*Look for intelligence and judgment, and most critically,
a capacity to anticipate, to see around corners. Also look
for loyalty, integrity, a high energy drive, a balanced
ego and the drive to get things done.—Colin Powell,
Former US Secretary of State and Joint Chiefs of Staff*

The ability to anticipate is merely the ability to think about what could happen and/or what you know will probably happen. Using your knowledge will help you look into the future. When you start looking into the future, you can make predictions and alter your course of action. By using your powers of anticipation, you can avoid or reduce last-minute, unexpected surprises and emergencies.

What can you anticipate? Here are some common examples (remember, these *aren't* unexpected):

- busy times of the week/month/quarter/year
- traveling (preparing to travel and returning from a business trip or vacation)
- vacations (yours or a coworker's)
- tradeshows (preparation and following up after)
- visitors (business VIPs, family, news reporters)

- track record of reliability of family, friends, coworkers, clients, and vendors
- changes in your energy levels
- longwinded phone callers
- traffic
- needing extra time in your schedule when learning or doing something for the first time
- bad weather causing event or school cancellations
- sending out a lot of e-mails and getting a flurry or blizzard of responses
- approval processes

Michael, one of my clients, went on many sales appointments to generate business for his small marketing firm. In one of our meetings, Michael told me that his schedule would get out of control, especially after he returned to the office from a sales appointment. I asked him two questions: why, and was it typical? His response was that after his sales calls, he needed to put together a proposal for the prospective client. He needed to get some of his staff involved in developing the proposal. He also told me that, yes, indeed, this scenario was typical.

I suggested to Michael that, after arranging a sales meeting, he should block out time in his schedule for the follow-up proposal-generation piece and inform his staff about the meeting and that they would need to be available to him to work on the proposal. As a result, the process of responding on a timely basis went more smoothly. His staff was happy to have the heads-up, and he had more control over his calendar for his other work.

My client Sam knew that his colleague Liz was going on vacation in a few weeks. Because Sam covers for Liz when she is on vacation, his work would be impacted by her absence. In the past, Sam would wait for Liz to come to him to review what she needed Sam to do while she was out. Liz always waited until a day or two before she left to initiate a conversation.

Since Sam knew Liz's schedule in advance, he could ask Liz to schedule a meeting two weeks prior to her vacation to review her workload and what she could foresee as issues that would affect Sam. They continued to have periodic meetings up until Liz's departure date. Sam was able to anticipate the work that he needed to accomplish and plan for it in a methodical manner. This way, Liz's vacation had minimal impact on Sam. The new process worked out well for both Sam and Liz.

Next Steps

1. Look ahead in your calendar, anywhere from three days to three months, to identify what is on your horizon.
2. Ask yourself, "What do I already know typically happens because of these occurrences?"
3. Determine what steps you can take to help remedy the negative impact of these events.
4. Decide what contingency planning you can do to positively change the typical outcome.
5. Enter your action steps into the task list on your planner or calendar.

B

Break It Down

Break it down: to clarify, disentangle, get down to basics, order, put in a nutshell, put one straight, reduce, spell out, unscramble

While intelligent people can often simplify the complex, a fool is more likely to complicate the simple.—Dr. Gerald W. Grumet, American psychiatrist

Breaking a task down into small, bite-size pieces is one way to simplify what you need to do. Understanding the added value in breaking something down will make a difference in how you view planning. It becomes easier to do the following:

- Set smaller objectives.
- Determine how much time something will take to do.
- Assess how to react to an interruption, determining whether to stop or continue with what you're doing or whether you can complete a small milestone before reacting to the interruption.
- Pick up from where you left off if you do react or respond to an interruption.
- Procrastinate less.
- Feel a sense of accomplishment.
- Improve communications with your staff, manager, family, friends, and children.

My client Debbie tended to make the smallest project into something overwhelming. Not only would this contribute to her procrastinating, but it also added to her stress. She was the secretary to a bank president and needed to complete projects that he requested on time.

During one of our coaching sessions, Debbie was talking about a *big* project that she needed to do. I asked her how long she thought it would take to complete. She told me that it would probably take three weeks.

I asked her to break the project down into bite-size doable

pieces. She listed each and every action item. After she completed her list, I asked her to write down, next to each item, the length of time she thought each action would take. Next, I had her add up the total number of hours.

She was astounded when she realized the project would take only three hours to complete! She had built up this *big* project in her mind without having a true sense of what it was really going to take to get it done. Debbie realized that when she broke it down, the project became clearer, more doable, and less stressful.

Shelly, another client, told me that her staff started to duck every time they saw her coming. Since she started breaking down her projects, she has been able to successfully offload tasks to her team. After she breaks her work down, she simultaneously sees what she really *needs* to be working on and what someone else on her team *could* be doing. She is able to get more work done and do less of it.

A third client, Fred, didn't look forward to weekly meetings with his manager. He never felt prepared and always scrambled to get his notes together for the meeting. After he started breaking his work down, he was able to communicate what his manager needed to know. He was able to tell his manager what he'd been working on, what he had left to do, and what obstacles he could foresee that could affect a deadline. Not only did Fred go into his meeting with more confidence, his manager felt that Fred was on top of his work.

Breaking Things Down

How do you start to break things down? Breaking things down is really creating a to-do list for something that potentially has several actions attached to it. It's a matter of figuring out what small steps need to be done to get the whole task completed, or of identifying at least the first few steps for getting the task started. The breaking-down process is outlined below using the task of choosing a caterer for an event.

Research
1. Go online and do a search for caterers.
2. E-mail friends and colleagues asking for recommendations.
3. Review the information and narrow down the choices.

Contact caterer
1. Prepare a list of questions.
2. Make the calls.
3. Determine next steps.

A key to each of these action steps is scheduling them into the task list on your planner or calendar.

Next Steps

1. Take a project or an item from your to-do list that has overstayed its welcome.
2. Ask yourself, "How can I break this down into smaller, more doable pieces?"
3. Write down the smaller components that you identify.
4. Turn each of the components into an action step.
5. Determine when you will take the first action, second action, and so on until all actions are completed.
6. Enter the action on the appropriate date in your planner or calendar.

Bonus B

Block Out Time

Block out time: take a quantity, portion, or section as a unit to be dealt with at one time, that time

This time, like all times, is a very good one, if we but know what to do with it. —Ralph Waldo Emerson, American poet

Blocking out time or scheduling an appointment with oneself is certainly not a new idea. Unfortunately, the result of putting *you* in your planner or calendar is that it becomes time we easily give up to someone else or something else. Through the years, I've seen this happen to many of my clients on their initial go-round with blocking out time.

Let's look at slightly changing how you block out time to get better results. When blocking out time or creating focus areas, the key ingredient to making it work is to be specific with what you intend to do with the time and put that specific intention into the task list on your planner or calendar so that you see it.

It's not enough to block out "project time" or "strategic planning time." You need to be able to see the specific task you want to accomplish in your block of time. In that way, you can make better decisions about whether to relinquish the time to someone or something else. Having something specific that needs to get done gives the time more importance than just a block for "administrative work," for example.

Do you stop what you're doing if asked to take care of something else, or do you continue with your plan? Once you have specific action items connected to your block of time, you will be able to make a more informed decision based on what you need to accomplish. You can now weigh which activity should take precedence. When you have specific time blocked out but no specified objective, it's very easy to give your time away.

When I was working with Jacob, a senior vice president at an engineering firm, I strongly suggested that he block out time for specific work he needed to get done. The caveat was that he needed to be specific when he blocked out, say, Tuesday morning from eight to nine thirty to get proposals out.

His solution was to schedule proposals as a recurring blocked activity. As he concluded his Tuesday morning work on his proposals, he looked at the next week's block of time and determined what he would specifically be working on during that time. In other words, he identified what milestone—meaning significant activity—needed to be accomplished on a proposal at that time. Milestones included budget, proposal overview, and personnel biographies involved in the project. He attached specific action items he would he need to do to achieve his milestones.

If planning a week ahead wasn't possible because there was uncertainty about what he needed to work on the following week, he became disciplined about entering the information once he was sure.

The process of blocking time out is similar to what happens when you begin to dig a hole on a beach with soft sand. As you start to dig, the sand immediately fills in the hole. As you keep digging, sand still fills in. Placing an object in the sand where you want to dig the hole will make it easier to maintain the integrity of the hole. The same is true with time. You need to block the time out in order to preserve it. If you don't, it will easily get filled in with other stuff.

Don't let "stuff" fill time you've blocked out.

Here are some examples of possible focus areas for blocks of time.

At work:
- reports
- paying or recording expenses
- scheduling meetings/preparing for meetings
- mentoring/coaching
- learning/training (yourself or others)
- administrative paperwork
- strategic planning
- e-mail
- responding to requests
- projects
- meetings with specific people or your team
- priority time (the time of day you focus on a priority activity)
- social media (LinkedIn, Facebook, Twitter)

At home:
- specific chores, such as laundry, cleaning, or grocery shopping
- exercising
- reading
- writing
- getting in touch with family or friends (by phone, Skype, or e-mail)
- going out with family or friends
- spending time at the library
- taking a class/doing homework or studying
- creative projects (painting, sculpting, crafts)
- vacation
- fixing up your house/house projects

- social media (Facebook, Pinterest, LinkedIn)
- hobbies

Figure out how much time each day, week, or month you want to spend on a specific focus area or a few focus areas. Not every minute of every day should be scheduled. Flexibility is key to working your focus areas smartly.

Determine an area that you need or want to focus on. Is it a daily, weekly, or monthly activity? A focus area will help ensure that either you have time scheduled for this important activity or that if the day gets off course, you can shift things around to make sure that the things you want to do get done.

White Space

White space is unscheduled time. Many of my clients, when they start to determine focus areas and start blocking out time, take it to an extreme, blocking out every minute of each day with a specific activity. The danger in blocking out time to the extreme is that it doesn't leave room for flexibility and unexpected occurrences. The unexpected will happen. When you begin the process of blocking out time, start with one or two focus areas and work them into your schedule. Then assess and see if it makes sense to add another focus area. But don't overcrowd your day.

Next Steps

1. Choose an activity you would like to focus on, or one you think that blocking time out would help you get to.
2. Determine how much time each day, week, or month you need for the activity.
3. Take a look at your planner or calendar, even if it's not completely up to date.

4. What day of the week and time of day makes sense to block out for this activity?
5. Be realistic—don't just block the time out without giving it some thought and anticipating obstacles.
6. Block out the time and enter it into your planner or calendar.
7. Write one or more specific action items you want to compete within the time you blocked out in your planner or calendar.

C

Clutter Traps

**Clutter: a number of things
scattered in disorder; jumble**

*Three Rules of Work: Out of clutter find simplicity; from
discord find harmony; in the middle of difficulty lies
opportunity.*—Albert Einstein, *German-born physicist*

Who has time to be organized? Nooks, crannies, and surface areas are to clutter as static cling is to clothing. Whether it's in an office, cubicle, or kitchen table, it doesn't matter—paper doesn't discriminate. Information comes at us via mail, e-mail, or written notes taken during a meeting. While watching TV or surfing the Internet, we jot something down on a piece of paper or print out information that we've found. The temptation is to put the paper somewhere, "just for now," and before you know it, you've created paper traps. The same holds true for *things*.

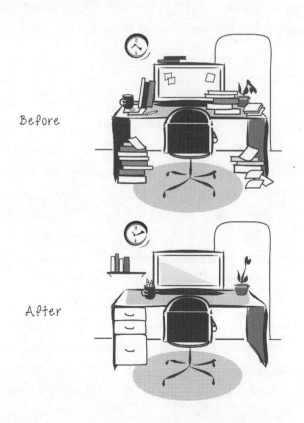

Before

After

We collect information and stuff. Think about how many times in a week you ask yourself or hear someone else ask, "Where's my _____," or "Have you seen my _____," or "Do you remember where we put _____?" How much time is wasted looking for things? How often do you rush to get someplace because you've spent unplanned time looking for your keys, jacket, sunglasses, or whatever you need to get out the door?

Before You Begin

Think about how you want to organize, and write it out on paper. For example, "The top file drawer in my office is dedicated to my projects. The middle drawer in my kitchen near the stove is for spices." Before you start emptying things out, have a thought-out written plan in place.

How to Begin

Begin by streamlining and simplifying. Clean up surface clutter, and you will feel instant gratification. It becomes visually pleasing to see what was once cluttered now nice and neat. But it's just as important to tackle the clutter in drawers or cabinets; even though you can't see it, you know it's disorganized.

Before you start, have the following supplies available:

- *Storage containers or cardboard boxes.* Where you plan to keep things will determine the type of container to purchase. If you will be storing papers in an attic or basement where there's a threat of water damage or moisture, plastic is preferable. Plastic also prevents papers from becoming musty, brittle, and discolored.
- *Labels and markers.* Make sure you buy labels that will

stick to the surface of your container, and don't forget dark-color markers.

- *File folders.* As you go through your papers, you may find information that you want to file. Instead of creating a pile of papers to file later, create file folders in advance and file as you go through your papers. This avoids double-handling of papers.
- *Trash bags/recycle bins.* You may actually find paper and things to throw away.
- *Donate.* As encouragement to sort through things, have preset donation boxes or bags at the ready. For example, put a box or bag on the floor of a clothes closet especially for clothing and accessories.

DAFT

DAFT is a method of sorting through your papers and clutter to help you decide what to do with it. The letters stand for the following:

- *Distribute or delegate.* Give it to the person who should have it.
- *Action.* Attach a task to the clutter by asking, "What is the next action I need to take?" For example, you receive an invitation and need to RSVP. Decide when you will reply and put the to-do in the task list on your planner or calendar (electronic or paper) task list.
- *File it* or put it away (and do it now!).
- *Throw it away.* Note that the wastebasket is your friend— it is like a pet and needs to be fed.

Let's take a closer look at that last item, "throw it away." Being able to throw things away tends to be one of the most problematic steps in getting rid of clutter. When establishing criteria for throwing things away, ask yourself the following questions:

- Do I really need this?
- Will I ever look at it, use it, or wear it again … really?
- Can I get it from another source (Internet, library, or other packrats)?
- Does it require a response?
- Will keeping this help me accomplish my goals and tasks, or further my career?
- Will it help my customers/clients, associates, or family?

Answering no to any of these questions is a good indication that it's time for an item to go.

Get Set

The bigger you make any cleanup project in your mind, the more difficult it will be to even get started, and the easier it will be to procrastinate. So start by scheduling small blocks of time, let's say twenty to thirty minutes. When you sit down to clean out a drawer, closet, cabinet, or shelf, have a specific target—for example, second drawer of the filing cabinet, top shelf of the closet.

If you are working on a drawer or shelf, remove all the contents. This makes it easier to go through all the items. To clean up the top of your desk, arrange everything into piles. Start with one pile and go through each piece of paper. If the piece of paper or folder requires a next-step action, put it on your task list as a to-do.

Keep Going

As you continue on with this process, you will become more and more comfortable using the wastebasket. You will wonder why you kept things that you will never need again. Use your criteria over and over again to determine what to keep and what to toss.

Clutter Prevention

Now that you have a plan to reduce the clutter, keeping the clutter at bay is the next challenge. The solution is to always put your keys in the same place—a piece of advice that doesn't just apply to keys. It really can be applied to everything, so that when you need anything, you know where to find it. Yet how many of us misplace not only our keys but our eyeglasses, dry-cleaning slips, forms that need filling out … you name it, it's hiding from us.

"ALWAYS PUT YOUR KEYS IN THE SAME PLACE"

The secret to reducing these frustrating searches is to have a strategy that's easy to remember: **CHER** (not the singer):

- Convenient
- Habit
- Easy to maintain
- Resilient

In French, *cher* means expensive. Something that is truly expensive when wasted is time. By following CHER as you develop your strategy, you will save time by having a working system. You won't necessarily get rid of your clutter, but you will have a strategy for better managing your things. Let's look at each of the CHER elements in more detail.

Convenient

Finding a home for everything is easy, but if it isn't convenient, you're doomed.

You need to find a practical and convenient place to store the things you need regularly, such as keys, first-aid kits, clothes you or your children wear regularly, or pots that you use a lot.

Habit

Make putting things where they belong a habit or ritual. Be consistent, and you'll never wonder where you put something. Just say to yourself, *It's no big deal to put this where it belongs. I'm just going to do it...now!* or *Don't put it down, just put it away.*

Easy to maintain

Once you've made something a habit, you have less build-up of stuff; it no longer requires a lot of thought or time to put things away. The process becomes effortless.

Binders are a great example of something that's difficult to maintain. My client Janie loved using binders to hold information from meetings or committees. The problem was that every time she got new information, she had to take out of the binder, get the three-hole punch, open the binder rings, and put the document in the appropriate section. When we were discussing the merits (in her mind) of the binder and my concerns about the binder, the problem became clear. When I asked her, "If I pick up this binder, will papers that haven't been filed fall out?" she replied with a smirk, "Don't pick up my binder."

Even though a binder can keep information organized and "neat," for many it's difficult to maintain its organization. In this case, Janie would have been better off using file folders so that she could simply drop a piece of paper in the appropriate folder, easily and quickly.

Resilient over time

Your system will survive the test of time. Because it's resilient, you can update it, review it, and revisit it when something doesn't seem to be working. The goal is to have it work for the long haul.

Next Steps

1. On paper, figure out how you want to organize the space—where things should go, what makes practical sense.
2. Establish your criteria for throwing things away.
3. Determine what you want to work on: drawer, shelf, closet, section of your desk, file folder, or the space under your bed.
4. Schedule small blocks of time in your planner or calendar.
5. Write or input specifically what you want to accomplish during your block(s) of time.
6. Commit to the process.
7. Be consistent!

D

Delegate

**Delegate: entrust, give, hand
over, hold responsible for**

*Surround yourself with the best people you can find,
delegate authority, and don't interfere.—Ronald
Reagan, fortieth president of the United States*

several years ago, I checked in with numerous clients, many of whom had been promoted several times or more. I asked them, "To what do you attribute your move up the corporate ladder?" The number-one answer: delegating!

The ability to delegate is a powerful skill that can make the difference between staying where you are (which is great, if that's what you want) or earning promotions throughout your career. Many strategies in this chapter, though primarily for business use, can also be relevant at home, though much more informally. As you read, think about ways to apply the strategies in multiple areas of your life.

What I see when working with clients is the tendency to want to push back when I suggest that they need to delegate. I hear so many reasons not to delegate, including the following:

- "I can do everything myself—quicker, better, and without error." Really? Is there no one else capable of taking on additional responsibilities? If that's the case, why do you have these folks working for you?
- "I can't give my employees challenging assignments, never mind giving them enough latitude or authority to handle them." If that's true, how do you expect to keep your employees interested and vested members of your team?
- "I haven't asked my employee to do something like this (untried and untested). I don't know what will happen." Who knows, maybe they will surprise you and emerge as superstars on your team!
- "I know I'm doing work that someone else probably

should be doing and can do, but I've always done it and it's easy for me." Is this what you are being paid to do? Is this a good return on your company's investment? What work aren't you doing that you are being measured on in your performance review that only you can or should do?

- "I don't want to waste my time following up on something I've delegated; I have trouble keeping up with my own work. Now I need to chase people down to monitor their progress on what I've delegated!" As a good manager, you need to stay in the loop, but you shouldn't have to chase people down; when you effectively delegate, you should include a plan for follow-up.

- "I can't overburden my best employee." Don't overburden your best employee by always going to that individual with work. Other members of your team need to step up. It's up to you to prepare them for the work you intend to delegate.

The manager who is not assigning or delegating is not managing. Anytime you perform a task that someone else can do, you keep yourself from tasks that only you can do.

Delegating vs. Assigning a Task

Unfortunately, all too often, the difference between *delegating work* and *assigning a task* is misunderstood. When you delegate, strive to give an individual total responsibility for the work. You want your involvement to lessen over time as that employee takes more and more ownership. The work should be recurring and/or ongoing, such as a monthly report or part of a continuing project. In other words, the next time the work needs to be done, the employee just does it—you don't need to ask to have it done, because that person owns it.

Of course, even though the employee owns it, the work may ultimately be your responsibility. You may be the person who reports to your boss and is held responsible. Periodically ask to be apprised of progress or accomplishments by the owner.

Assigning work means asking someone to do a task. Once the task is done, it's done—no additional work is required. It may be asking someone to make a plane reservation or send an e-mail or make a phone call. It isn't recurring or ongoing. It's just a task.

Why Delegate?

The ability to be a good, effective delegator can have significant benefits that far outweigh any trepidation you may have about delegating. They include the following:

- You will accomplish more and meet deadlines more easily.
- Your team will become more involved and committed to the work.
- Effectively delegating work will make controlling the work flow straightforward.
- Employees grow, develop, and add value to your organization.
- Employee satisfaction increases.
- You have more time to do the things you should be doing—those things that only you can do.

The number-one reason to delegate is that delegating represents an investment in yourself and your career. You start to be seen as someone who can manage and lead people thoughtfully and with ease. The leaders of your company will see you as someone who knows how to work well with people, guiding and trusting the team to get the work done.

Six Keys to Delegating

There are six important elements to delegating:
1. Personal planning
2. Preparation
3. Communication
4. Commitment
5. Review
6. Feedback

Let's look at each of these in more detail.

Personal planning

Personal planning is the thinking that precedes delegating. This is when you determine what you should be delegating so you can spend your time on higher-priority work. It involves knowing and understanding what is on your plate and what can be passed on to someone else. This is the time to look ahead and see what is coming up so that you can involve someone else sooner rather than later. If you wait until the last minute as a deadline nears, you will, by default, become the best person to do the work.

Start thinking about what you do daily, monthly, quarterly, or yearly. Ask yourself, "What would I like to, and what should I remove from my plate?"

To help you identify work to delegate, see the illustration on pages 32 and 33.

Preparation

As you begin to look at the work you want to delegate, you need to identify who you believe is best-suited to take charge. Give it some thought. When you meet with staff, ask them what interests them. Are there certain areas they would like to focus on and take over? What opportunities have they wished they had been given but were overlooked?

Figure out if any training or special help is needed. If there is, then plan how and when that help or training will be provided. This is also a good time to determine the objectives of what you are delegating. A formula that will help you as you begin is TimeFinder's GPS.

GPS usually stands for *global positioning system*, the navigation system that gets us from one place to another. When delegating, GPS can help keep you and the person to whom you are delegating on track. In this case, GPS stands for: Goal, Purpose, and Scope.

- *Goal*. Determine the objectives and set the goals. What does the work you are delegating look like when it's completed?

- *Purpose*. Understand the purpose and the "why" of any work in which you are involving someone. That's how you get buy-in to a project. Explain how the work you are delegating fits into the bigger picture of the team or company goals.

- *Scope*. What can you share? Examples include deadline, format, who will see it (audience), budget, available resources (people or information), decision-making authority, who else is involved, capital, equipment, facilities, standards, and your involvement.

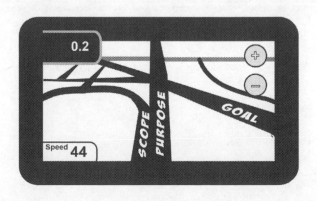

— Identifying Work to Delegate —

Projects	Deadlines	Delegate To?	Next Steps and Date

Ongoing Work	Delegate To?	Next Steps and Date

It's absolutely essential when working with your team—whether it's your work team, family team, or any team—that the goal, purpose, and scope are communicated clearly and understood by all involved. You must know what is expected of an individual, when it's expected, and how best to employ people to obtain the desired results. This means assigning or delegating work in a planned and thoughtful way. The quality of your preparation will determine the success of a project or task. Managers who ignore the personal planning and preparation steps are usually those who are less motivating and will lose productivity and the confidence of their team.

Because you may find pushback when delegating, part of your preparation must be to think about and identify possible objections that an employee or team member may raise. This must be done prior to the meeting, not in the moment. You must be ready to counter the objections in a way that is calm and firm. If you aren't prepared, you could look like a "deer in the headlights" and not be able to handle the objections in a professional, attentive way.

Communication

The heart of delegating is the interaction between you and the person to whom you are giving responsibility. Delegating isn't pushing the work down. It's a process that takes time and careful consideration. Make the time. Take the time. Don't delegate if you are rushed or in the midst of a crisis.

Delegating requires open communication. When communication is lacking or the quality of your relationship with team members isn't strong, trust will be missing on both sides. Without good communication, you're likely to end up with lack of motivation, work done incorrectly, and frustration for all involved.

Your attitude, knowledge, and approach will directly

influence the success of each and every project you are managing and all of the work you've delegated that is ultimately your responsibility. Start by setting standards with the following steps:

1. Describe the project and results expected as fully as possible. Pass on all information as needed or let team members know where they can obtain necessary information.

2. Agree on standards of performance and timetables. The scope of the assignment has already been determined, but you want input on standards, including a reasonable timetable for completion of the work.

3. Determine needed training or special help and when it will be provided. Ask what information or training team members feel is needed to be successful.

4. Define parameters and resources, including the scope as discussed earlier. Depending on the individual and your confidence in his or her work, it may be a good idea to ask for a written action plan, including steps and a timeline for accomplishing the work.

5. Be clear on how much decision-making authority you are delegating. How much will you let the individual do on his or her own? You can give absolutely no authority or total authority to run with it. And of course, there are levels in the middle, such as, "Do what needs to be done but make sure you report the results to me." The point is that you must communicate this information; you can't expect the employee to presume.

Next, formulate a communications plan. Start by explaining how you want to receive updates. Each individual contributor's action plan should have a component that specifically outlines the what, how, and when of the updates and what information should be shared on the project status, including whether the work is on schedule to be completed by deadline, whether you need to intervene in any way, and what obstacles may get in the way of meeting the deadline. Specify how the information is to be communicated: e-mail, telephone call, face-to-face meeting or team meeting. Determine when and how often information will be shared.

A communication plan that is understood and in place helps reduce time spent chasing down information and eliminates unpleasant surprises, such as missed deadlines. As you receive updates, make sure you follow up with questions. Don't just ask, "So how's it going?" This implies that you are only interested in one answer—"Fine!"—or that you are asking because you should but you don't really want to get into a discussion about it. When someone asks you how you're doing, how often do you actually talk about how you are *really* doing?

Instead, ask questions to which you need answers. These may include the following:

- "What is working well?"
- "What might you/we want to do differently?"
- "What obstacles have you run across?"
- "How are you planning to resolve that issue?"
- "What have you accomplished since our last meeting?"
- "What remains undone?"

Take on the role of adviser and offer options if asked. One way to make a conversation go badly is to be patronizing or tell others what to do. The implication is that you don't trust their abilities. The result: they will get frustrated and lose confidence in their abilities too, or decide to rely on you—thus negating the effectiveness of the delegation.

To avoid this, use a simple phrase when you make a suggestion, such as, "I know you know this," "You've probably already thought of this," or "What questions can I answer for you?" This keeps you from sounding condescending. The conversation remains professional.

Commitment

Commitment can't be forced. It usually develops through a feeling of involvement. People increase their commitment to a team when they are allowed to contribute to its success. Creating ownership is essential.

In an article for TLNT.com entitled "Company Goals: Do Your Employees Have a 'Line of Sight' to them?," Jacque Vilet writes, "There's a famous story from the early days of the space race. President John F. Kennedy was visiting NASA headquarters for the first time, in 1961. While touring the facility, he introduced himself to a janitor who was mopping the floor and asked him what he did at NASA. The janitor replied, "I'm helping put a man on the moon!" The man's response revealed that he was committed and part of the team. Show your team how their responsibilities are interwoven. You are all relying on each other.

Review

Review your process; get input from your team. What is working in how you delegate? What improvements can you make? Ask! You need to know in order to be more effective.

Feedback

As important as it is for you to get feedback, you must also give feedback. There are two different kinds of feedback: appreciation and advice (coaching).

Appreciation means expressing gratitude or approval for someone's effort. We all have an emotional need to be appreciated. Showing appreciation early and often boosts people's mood and commitment. However, it's important, when expressing appreciation, that it's specific and sincere. Telling some that they're doing "a great job" is empty. Telling someone that the way he or she set up the presentation on a report was clear to everyone in the meeting is specific and meaningful. Even when the results are less than desirable, you can still show appreciation. I heard a story about a man who rushed into the water to help save someone who was drowning. Even though the individual he was trying to save drowned, the man deserved appreciation for his efforts.

Advice focuses on improving performance. The conversation should be impersonal. You are more likely to get good work if you focus on how to improve the work rather than improving the person. It helps to begin by asking questions so you can understand what the person was trying to do. Reinforce what worked well and ask what he or she thinks could have been done differently. During the conversation, share your advice. Look for and praise success. Frame the suggestions positively: do more X and less Y. For example, you might say, "It was obvious to me that you worked extremely hard in putting your presentation together. If you speak more on your topic and rely less on the slides, your message will be more easily understood."

To be a good manager, it's necessary to let go and let others grow. Build confidence and display trust!

Next Steps

1. Determine what you will delegate, to whom you will delegate, and why you are choosing this person.
2. Be prepared to share the goal, purpose, and scope (GPS)
3. Know your key expectations/standards and be able to communicate them.

4. Think through all the possible objections and be able to thoughtfully counter them.
5. Define the amount of authority you are allowing.
6. Develop a communication plan.
7. Prepare any additional information.
8. Once you are prepared, schedule a meeting.
9. Ask for input from the individual or individuals to whom you are delegating—they are a key part of the process.
10. *Be prepared!*

E

Evaluate

Evaluate: assess; to judge or determine the significance, worth, or quality of

I am a scholar of life. Every night before I go to sleep, I analyze every detail of what I did that day. I evaluate things and people, which helps me avoid mistakes.—Compay Segundo, Cuban musician

We are all going at such a fast pace, trying to get things done or get someplace. We are always on the go, and too often we don't take time to stop and evaluate what we are doing, how we are doing it, what is working, and what we could improve upon.

Many of us take a look back right around New Year's. This seems to be a time to reflect on the past year and make resolutions to improve the year ahead. It's the time for a life makeover. Unfortunately, resolutions are short-lived, even with good intentions. When there is no substantive plan attached, they tend to fall by the wayside until the next year when the cycle begins anew and in earnest.

Taking a step back allows you the opportunity to improve the things that are impediments to your productivity, goals, or life in general. Begin by choosing something you want to improve. It could be a situation that didn't turn out the way you wanted, a recurring process that's not efficient or effective, or even something simple that only needs some refinement. Once you've chosen something to work on, ask yourself the following:

- What are the issues that contribute to it not working?
- What are some causes? In other words, why is this happening?
- What are some possible approaches to improving the situation?
- What are the step(s) needed to make this improvement?

Take a good hard look at the answers to these questions. What areas for change/improvement can you control? Which ones are totally out of your control? In her book *I Could Do Anything If I Only Knew What It Was: How to Discover What You Really Want and How to Get It*, author Barbara Sher writes, "It's essential to distinguish between events that are really beyond your control and events you caused yourself." Are there events that you don't think you have control over? Perhaps if you delve a little further, you'll find that you have the ability to make changes toward improvement.

All too often, I hear—and you probably hear this as well, either from yourself or others—"There's nothing I can do about it; it's out of my hands." Sometimes this is indeed the case, but many times, it's just easier to go along and let things happen than to put in the extra effort to make things better.

Many years after I started TimeFinder and began offering half-day workshops, I noticed a trend: my clients were telling me they were having difficulty getting employees to commit to the daylong training and half-day training programs they offered. I took a step back and asked myself the four evaluation questions above. That exercise led me to offer programs in varying lengths, ranging from one to two hours.

Realizing that there is a difference in approach in a short program as opposed to a half-day workshop, I had to be prepared to speak about the pros of each and focus on the value to my clients' employees. This opened up new possibilities for me and my clients.

We do these kinds of evaluations all the time when we recognize that something isn't working. However, a difference occurs when you take the steps to figure out *why* and strategize possible remedies for making something better. Just thinking about something doesn't make it happen; taking the time to think it through and really work it out does.

Time taken to evaluate situations is time well spent. It keeps you at the top of your game, not lulled into complacency. This thoughtful process is a great way to regularly make adjustments and changes and not let a lot of things build up that need addressing.

Next Steps

1. Identify something that isn't working for you. It could be a family or work routine, the way you exercise, a procedure, or the route you take to get from one place to another.
2. Review the steps for evaluating the issue.
3. What is the first step toward making an improvement?
4. Take that first step.

F

Focus

Focus: to concentrate

Nothing can add more power to your life than concentrating all your energies on a limited set of targets.—Nido Qubein, author and businessman

Y ou wake up. You intend to have a truly productive day. You have lots on your to-do list, but it's manageable. And then *it* happens. *It* is what begins to get your day off track.

Unplanned and unscheduled events can easily pull you away from what you hoped to get done. You quickly start to see your optimism for a focused day diminishing. However, through self-examination, you may begin to see what you do to contribute to your own downward spiral. Once you start to reduce the activities that steer you off course, the uncontrolled, unexpected occurrences won't get in the way of your concerted and concentrated effort to get things done. You'll learn to stay focused as you complete the tasks on your list.

Off and On Track

Jackie had set her priorities for the day. Then she received a message from a partner in her firm asking about billing. The billing work was to be completed by the end of the pay period, which was within the next couple of days. Jackie was frustrated that she had to rearrange her day to take care of this matter.

At first glance, it looks as if the partner put the monkey wrench into Jackie's day. But in fact, Jackie threw her own day off track. She knows that the billing deadline is the same each month. Jackie should have worked on the billing before the partner intervened. If she had planned to work on the billing in order to meet the deadline, she could have avoided rearranging her priorities and been less frustrated (which can and usually does impact focus).

David, a tax accountant, planned to review a tax return when he arrived at work. He began his day by reading an e-mail about a new tax law. He updated his calendar, input billing time, and then was ready to review the tax return. A colleague came to him needing some help doing research. He did the research and checked on the status of another return that wasn't completed (the preparer was going on vacation). He needed to find another preparer, and the story goes on. David never reviewed the tax return that day.

David's day could have been productive if he made the following adjustments:

1. Review the tax return before doing anything else, since it was his top priority.
2. When his colleague needs help, choose one of the following:
    - help his colleague because he was well into completing the review of the tax return and had time and focus available
    - stay focused on completing the return and offer to help the colleague later
    - direct the colleague to someone else
3. When assigning the tax-return review, ask if the preparer would have difficulty meeting the deadline. Once David learned that the preparer was going on vacation, he could have found someone else to review it.
4. Read about the new tax law at a more appropriate time.

The following are some common traps that can cause a loss of focus and decrease productivity:

- engaging with social media and surfing the Internet without clear objectives
- spending time on trivia and not enough time on priorities

- acting in a reactive manner to requests for help (dropping your task at hand)
- being blindsided by not anticipating what's on the horizon
- reading e-mail before doing anything else
- socializing too long with colleagues
- not having prepared a written plan for the day
- doing someone else's job
- scheduling/attending early-morning in-house meetings

Take a step back and scrutinize your day. Determine your contribution to getting your day off track and make one change. Then move on.

When you find that you aren't doing what you had planned and you've lost focus, stop in your tracks. It's time to regroup. As the American author William Arthur Ward said: "The pessimist complains about the wind. The optimist expects it to change. The realist adjusts the sails." Adjust your sails, set your course, and keep your focus.

Next Steps

1. Take a recess break (just like in elementary school): go for a walk, change location, and clear your head for five minutes.
2. Reevaluate your to-do list by reviewing what needs to be done, creating a timeline to completion, reprioritizing, anticipating problems, and delegating if possible and appropriate.
3. Get someone else's perspective and input on how to proceed.
4. Do something easy and simple, and then go back to something more important or challenging.

G

Goals

Goal: the result or achievement toward which effort is directed; aim; end result

Setting a goal is not the main thing. It is deciding how you will go about achieving it and staying with that plan.
—Tom Landry, American football player and coach

D r. Robert Schuller, the retired American evangelist, asks, "What would you attempt to do if you knew you could not fail?"

Our dreams often become clouded when we start facing reality. And it's too often the case that reality has nothing to do with someone not reaching his or her goal. The thought of turning an idea into an action plan can become so overwhelming that stop signs start filling our heads with all the reasons we can't do something. In this section, we turn those intangible, difficult-to-conceive goals into actions that you *can* accomplish.

Even if you have never been a goal-setter before, once you start to write, think, and talk about your goals on an ongoing basis, you will almost immediately see a dramatic improvement in your levels of performance and achievement. The subconscious mind goes to work to bring the goal to the forefront of your thinking and starts you on your way to achieving it.

According to *Think and Grow Rich* author Napoleon Hill, desire, faith, imagination, persistence, and organized planning are a few of the key components of success. I'll add one of my own: attitude. Your success belongs to you, and you choose how you define it.

Why Set Goals?

Here's a quick and easy exercise to help demonstrate the value of setting goals. Stand up and twist your upper torso to the right as far around as you can go without hurting yourself. Find a spot to look at on the wall when you can't twist any farther. Untwist yourself and face forward. Do the same thing again, twisting back, but this time, go a tiny bit beyond where you stopped the first time you twisted.

Reach

Were you able to go beyond your original limit? Every time I have asked clients to do this exercise, they are able to go a little bit further than their initial stopping point. By setting a goal—in this case, twisting beyond your initial stopping point—you established direction, identified results, and to some extent intensified performance, pushing yourself to go beyond.

Not only does a goal establish the direction in which you want to go and help you identify results and intensify your performance, it also improves teamwork when you're working with others. Working as a team and understanding the goal puts all members on the same page and leaves little room for misunderstanding. All team members may not agree with the goal, but at least the goal is clear.

There are three different types of goals, and identifying which of the following you are setting helps to prioritize your goal's importance:

1. An *essential goal* is one that must be done. It's vital to

everyday activities that require completion and must be fulfilled to ensure successful results. Examples include meeting payroll, paying bills, creating a budget, stopping smoking, and losing weight.

2. A *problem-solving goal* is one that ought to be done. Problem-solving goals are derived from sources of problems that occur. They can be areas that need improvement, such as productivity, efficiency, or accident prevention. Other examples include getting a new computer, upgrading software, refinancing your home, improving fitness, or putting up a fence to prevent the dog from running away.

3. An *innovative goal* is one that you would like to do. This is a goal that will improve a current condition but isn't a problem that needs solving. It's making something that is good even better. It can be about identifying activities that will make something faster, cheaper, easier, or safer. It would most likely be about identifying something that you really want to do for *you*. Examples include writing a book, getting paid top dollar to be a professional speaker, mentoring a child, taking exotic vacations (or just taking vacations regularly), buying a sports car, or spending more time with family.

It is worth noting that there are times when the three types of goals can overlap. For example, it may be essential to lose weight for health reasons, which is also a problem-solving goal because you are out of breath a lot of the time because of your weight.

Identifying the type of goal makes it easier to prioritize what needs to be done first. The essential is the highest priority, problem-solving would come next, and innovative would be the least important. Innovative goals tend to be the ones we really want to do but put on the back burner.

Working to integrate an innovative goal into the day is important because it gives us the motivation to do something special, to accomplish something that may seem out of reach. It can become too easy to just let those goals fall by the wayside. Taking something that we can only imagine and turning it into tangible action can be exciting.

With any goal, it's important to be able to define it and understand what you want or need to accomplish.

Get SMART

Before you begin tackling a goal, a key question to ask is, "How can I clearly define my goal?" A goal needs to be well-defined. One of the best formulas for defining a goal is to make it SMART. I don't know who came up with the SMART formula, but it works and has worked for many people over many years.

Using the SMART formula can help narrow the scope of the goal. What does SMART stand for?

- Specific
- Measureable
- Action-oriented
- Realistic
- Time constraints

Here's how each of those elements breaks down:

- *Specific* goals are detailed with particular or exact focus. Examples include losing weight, improving customer-service ratings on response times, and learning a foreign language.

- *Measureable* goals have a standard for comparison—a specific and limited result like doing something better or more accurately or improvement year over year. Examples include losing ten pounds, increasing sales by 10 percent, and decreasing product returns by 27 percent.
- *Action-oriented* goals tell you what needs to be done to reach them. *Evaluate, inform, lose, decrease,* or *increase* are verbs that describe the action to be taken.
- *Realistic* goals ensure that what you want to accomplish is practical, achievable, and possible. For a goal to motivate, it must feel as though it can be met. There also must be a perceived need to achieve the goal. Challenging and realistic goals motivate and encourage higher levels of performance. If the goal is unrealistic, it becomes easy to give up. An example of an unrealistic goal would be running a marathon in two hours.
- *Time constraints* present a timeframe and a deadline to encourage you to stay on track, reaching milestone after milestone. Not having a deadline allows the procrastinator in you to put it off. There is no sense of time pressure or urgency to get it done. An example of a time constraint would be a requirement to complete the goal by January 31, 2015.

As you define your goal and make it SMART, really take a look at it. Is it clear? Are you sure about what you are trying to accomplish? One of the best ways to make sure your goal is clear is to share it with someone you trust to be supportive and honest with you.

When discussing your goal, you may realize that it isn't realistic—that is usually the biggest realization—or that it can't be measured the way you have described it. This is a great time to rethink and restate the goal so that it's SMART. The illustration shows some examples of SMART and not-so-SMART goals.

What are the differences between the "not-so-SMART" and "SMART" goals? The not-so-SMART goals are vague descriptions of desires, while the SMART goals are specific, measureable, action-oriented, realistic, and have a time constraint or deadline. They make it easier to begin to focus on them and get them done.

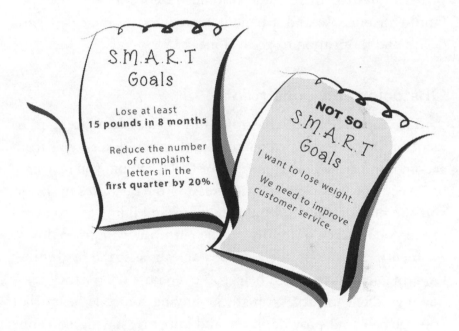

What's in It for You

People perform better when convinced that there are personal or professional benefits. Whether it's a business goal or a personal goal, you must identify the benefits and advantages if you want to adequately perform the tasks necessary to achieve the goal.

One element that makes a big difference in how you

approach the goal is acknowledging why accomplishing the goal is important to you. If it's a company goal you need to work on, determine how the company will directly benefit from achieving the goal and how you will directly benefit as well. You must be able to see "what's in it for me."

The other piece in this equation could be the importance of the goal to someone else who is important to you—your family, spouse, partner, friend, or favorite charity. Will you be able to travel more, go out to eat more, or spend more time with your children? Is there an additional benefit for someone else? Finding a purpose and a benefit for your goal increases your desire and motivation to get it done.

Obstacles and Constraints

The flip side to all of this, and a necessary step, is to identify the obstacles or constraints that could keep you from accomplishing the goal. Ignoring obstacles can put you in a state of "stuck" or frustration. By addressing the obstacles up front, you can put together contingency plans and find ways to avoid getting sidetracked or totally off the path you want to go down.

Identifying the obstacle or obstacles is just the beginning. Creating actions that will help you overcome the obstacles is a key ingredient to success. Just like having someone hear what your goal is and provide input and support, having someone help you look at ways to overcome potential obstacles, can make the difference between success and procrastination.

The obstacles must be put into tangible terms. For example, you might say, "I just don't have the money" or "This isn't the right time." But what do those really mean?

During one of my "Go for It! Going for the Goal!" workshops, a participant shared her goal of going back to school to get an advanced degree. When we got to discussing the obstacles, she said she didn't have the funds to pay for it. The discussion that ensued helped her create an action plan that included meeting with a financial planner and looking at financial-aid options. She had clearly defined steps to begin to overcome her obstacle.

Goal » Project

In many situations, when you begin to define your goal, you will identify smaller goals derived from the larger goal. Let's take the example of losing twenty pounds. As you begin to put your plan together, you may realize that there are subgoals, such as eating goals or exercise goals or going-to-the-gym goals or contacting a weight-loss program goals. These are key to the success of the overall goal of losing twenty pounds.

It becomes easier to work with these smaller goals if you think of them as projects. Look at each and create an action plan, just as you would for any other project you are working on. Once you start to break these projects down into bite-size, doable to-dos, you can integrate them into your daily plan by putting them on your to-do list.

The action plan needs to define the to-dos to accomplish the project. Having a timeframe for when to complete the project is helpful, but more important is deciding when you will work on the to-dos, scheduling them into the task list on your planner or calendar and then sticking to the schedule.

There's one more vital piece that is part of accomplishing your goal, and that is really *wanting* to make it happen. Before creating your action plan, perform the TimeFinder Honesty and Reality Check. You must say *yes* to the following questions.

1. Do I really want to make it happen?
2. Am I being realistic?
3. If necessary, am I willing to work at it over a period of time?

4. Am I willing to reevaluate and make adjustments to my current activities?

Dream and Vision Board

Another method for approaching goals is to create a dream and vision board to help you begin to visualize your goal through pictures and words. These are images that you can have right in front of you every day as a reminder of your goals. When you see the board, it motivates you to take the actions needed to make your dream a reality.

There are many ways to make a board. One is with magazines, a piece of construction paper, scissors, and glue sticks. Look through a magazine and choose pictures and words that represent your goal or what motivates you, or just how you are feeling about accomplishing your goal. Place the pictures and words on the construction paper in a way that pleases you.

CREATE YOUR DREAM AND VISION BOARD

Another method is to use technology to help you create your board. I have created these both on paper and online. For the virtual board, I used Animoto (www.animoto.com) and uploaded pictures and images I found through Google. I chose motivating words, added music, and created something that I watch every day.

There are companies that sell downloadable software for creating a vision board. You can find these companies by doing a Google search on "dream and vision board."

Working on Your Goals

When working on your goals, keep the process simple. Find ways to integrate the actions into your daily plan. Until you spend some time looking at what you want or need to accomplish and determine the means to accomplish it, it will look overwhelming and, possibly, monstrous.

Your goal must be broken down into bite-size doable pieces. It's easy to procrastinate when something seems huge. You tell yourself you're waiting for that big chunk of time to work on it, or just the right time. The right time may never happen, so you'll need to make it happen, even if you can only carve out small chunks of time.

Commit to take action. All in all, you can plan and plan and plan, but without action, plans are meaningless. As American football coach Lou Holtz said, "Ability is what you're capable of doing. Motivation determines what you do. Attitude determines how well you do it."

Keep your motivation at the forefront of your mind. It's what will drive you even when you think you can't get there. Remember, each day you are that much closer to achieving your goal.

Next Steps

1. Decide on a goal.
2. Define the goal and make it SMART.
3. Determine what's in it for you—why is this goal important to you?
4. Understand and figure out how to overcome the likely obstacles you will face.
5. Take the Honesty and Reality Check to make sure you are committed to the goal.
6. Turn the goal into a project.
7. Create an action plan for the project.
8. Incorporate the action plan into your daily to-do list.
9. Do it!

H

Help

Help: to give or provide what is necessary to accomplish a task or satisfy a need; contribute strength or means to; render assistance to

A little boy was having difficulty lifting a heavy stone. His father came along just then. Noting the boy's failure, he asked, "Are you using all your strength?"

"Yes, I am," the little boy said impatiently.

"No, you are not," the father answered. "I am right here, just waiting, and you haven't asked me to help you."—Author Unknown

I f you have difficulty asking people for help, you may want to start looking at the value in asking for help from various perspectives. Looking at asking for help as a sign of weakness or as an acknowledgment that you are unable to do something on your own will only leave you struggling to complete whatever challenge is set before you.

For some people, asking for help comes very easily, almost too easily. It can be a sign of laziness, just not wanting to make an effort to get something done.

On the other side is the person who, to a fault, won't ask for help. In some cases, it's pride, in other cases it may be not wanting to appear weak, incapable, unable, or not smart enough to do what they've been asked to do or even volunteered to do. This may be especially true when a job is on the line or an employment market is tough. Being seen as able and capable could make the difference between having your job or losing it.

However, those who ask for help can be seen as able because they want to create positive outcomes. In some instances, asking for help is a way to reduce chaos that has surfaced.

My client Sarah was the managing partner and owner of her accounting firm. She had two other partners, and employees relied upon her. She was the rock of the firm. When Sarah's husband, Rob, became ill, she found it necessary to get help in many different ways. Rob was ill for over two years. The first six months, he was at home, and then the next year and half, he was in and out of hospitals. Sarah told me, "The biggest problem is that you lose your focus. It's really hard with extended periods of stress; I really had to keep my focus on all fronts."

Many of Rob's problems required that Sarah get up to speed

on medical issues, Medicaid, and Medicare, all which were totally foreign to her. Much of it she had to learn during tax season. Sarah said, "My life was like an out-of-control speeding train. At some point I had put the brakes on, get off for a minute and say, 'Okay, I'm going to get my PDA [personal digital assistant] working *for* me, as opposed to against me.' There was a time when it was demanding attention from me rather than me getting use out of it. So I had to hone my tools. That took some of the stress off."

Sarah met with her partners and explained that she needed them to step up to the plate during this difficult time. She also hired someone to deal with the Medicare and Medicaid stuff. She explained that hiring an expert in that area meant she didn't have to learn all the details. The person she hired was also a nurse, and that helped her understand her husband's medical issues. Sarah also got Rob's physician to agree to use e-mail with her so that when she had a question, she could ask and get an answer.

Sarah said, "I essentially pulled in every resource I could figure out." Once her husband was able to come home, Sarah even hired someone to cook meals. Finally, she was able to stop enough to really get her focus back.

Sarah is savvy and very capable—one smart businesswoman. She recognized what help she needed and sought it out. By finding people to help her, she not only reduced her stress and increased her focus, but she also was able to be there for her husband. Now she could focus on him during her visits and not be distracted by worries about extraneous things.

Unfortunately, too often we see colleagues or friends ask for help without trying to figure out if they can resolve a situation on their own. These people simply rely too much on others. If you see people using others and causing negative feelings, you may think to yourself that you don't want to be like that person.

You don't want to be seen as someone who causes someone else to be inconvenienced. The fine line is recognizing when asking for help is a necessity and most other options don't exist.

When is it appropriate to ask for help? Look for the following signs:

- You're feeling so overwhelmed that it's like you're swimming against the tide.
- A missed deadline is imminent.
- You just don't know enough and need more information.
- You have reached capacity and feel you've done as much as you can on your own.
- Others need to take on more.
- When someone offered help to you initially, you turned it down.
- You know there are others more knowledgeable or better able to assist than you.
- Other things you are working on or are involved in are being compromised.

The bottom line is, ask for help when you really feel you need help. If you don't ask for it, you'll never receive it.

Next Steps

1. Recognize when you are struggling with something or could use some assistance or help with something.
2. Identify who can help you.
3. Determine the best way to approach the person so that you are comfortable asking for help.
4. Ask for help!

I

Itinerary

Itinerary: a line of travel; route

We face a particularly busy itinerary this year and it's important that we plan and pace ourselves for each challenge.—Stephen Kenny, Irish footballer and manager

After we make our reservations to travel by air, the airline sends us an itinerary for our journey that includes departure time and city, arrival time and city, and any stopovers along the way. If our travel is more extensive, we are given more details, which could include hotel, car rental, and tours. These particulars help ensure that we are where we need to be when we need to be there so as not to miss a flight, ship, or outing.

If you tend to be late for meetings, child pickups, or deadlines, or if you get off track by doing "one more thing" or just not thinking ahead, creating an itinerary for yourself will help you stay the course.

An itinerary is more than a schedule; it's a map to get you from one event to the next, even if it means getting out of your house in the morning to get to work, arriving on time to pick up your son or daughter at a game, or being on time when meeting a friend for dinner.

Melissa, a mother of two, was always late. She was late for the train, late for work, late for meetings, late getting home from work—late. In order to address what was becoming a growing issue for both Melissa and her new manager, something had to be done.

I asked Melissa to write down her morning routine, from the time she woke up to the time she reached work.

Melissa's Original Morning Schedule
7:45: Wake up
7:45–8:15: Play with children

8:15–9:00: Shower, wash hair, pick out clothes, and get dressed
9:00–9:15: Talk to nanny (who arrives at 8:00)
9:15–9:30: Gather stuff up for work
9:30–9:45: Leave for fifteen-minute walk to train
9:45: Take train
10:15: Arrive at work late

The result of Melissa's lateness was that she would have to stay later at work, which threw the evening schedule off. The nanny needed to leave by six p.m., and the children should be eating dinner around six thirty. Instead, the nanny, who had her own family, stayed later, and the children were eating well after seven because Melissa made dinner when she got home.

We've all seen the ripple effect one event can cause. In Melissa's case, the trigger was not leaving for work earlier. A great technique to counter lateness is to work backward—figure out the absolute latest you can leave, and work through the events that lead up to that in reverse order. Moving backward through her day to the start, Melissa and I were able to determine the following:

- what time she needed to be at work
- what time the ideal train departed
- what time she had to leave the house to walk to the train
- what time she had to shower and dress
- how much playtime was realistic for her to spend with her children in the morning on a workday

Playtime was the toughest one to tackle, because Melissa cherished her time in the morning with her children.

Melissa decided to spend a little more time with her children but get up earlier to do so, understanding that she would have even more time with her children when she got home from work because she would be home earlier. This would result in a calmer, easier evening and bedtime routine. Melissa also realized that if she washed her hair and picked out her clothes the night before, she would save as much as thirty minutes in the morning.

The next step was to put times next to each item and then, critical to the process, examine the new itinerary to make sure it was realistic.

Melissa's Revised Morning Schedule
7:00: Wake up
7:00–7:45: Play with children
7:45–8:15: Shower and get dressed
8:15–8:30: Talk to nanny
8:30: Gather things up for work
8:40: Leave for fifteen-minute walk to train
9:00: Take train
9:30: Arrive at work early!

The new itinerary worked because of Melissa's willingness to get up a little earlier and follow the new morning schedule we created.

Now you may be asking yourself, "Do I need to do this every time I'm going to meet someone for dinner?" The short answer is, yes and no. It all depends on you and your track record. You need to decide when an itinerary, extensive or simple, is needed.

Creating an itinerary, figuring out when you need to leave, thinking about the obstacles that you may run into that could make you late—all of these are steps in the right direction. Look at your to-do list for the day. How will it impact your ability to leave on time? Do you tend to do "one last thing" before leaving? If so, you absolutely need to tell yourself that you won't do that—no matter what—and keep thinking about that throughout your day. Being stern with yourself forces you to focus on what's important: your priorities!

Jot down your itinerary for arriving at your dinner or meeting or whatever it may be. Work the itinerary backward to figure out what needs to happen for you to be on time, including what you need to avoid doing so that you aren't delayed.

This requires mind-set and determination in addition to the practical, realistic itinerary that you work out. The trick is to make that itinerary and stick to it!

Next Steps

1. Think about a situation that you would like to remedy regarding being late. The key here is, you have to want to fix it.
2. Write down your current itinerary.
3. Work it backward, starting with when you should arrive.
4. Determine what adjustments you need to make.
5. Rewrite a new and improved itinerary.
6. Follow it!

J

Jump-Start
Your Day

**Jump-start: to start or improve something
more quickly by giving it extra help**

*He does things to jump-start us. He is so active on the
defensive end anticipating, creating tips and steals, that he
acts as a catalyst for us and really gets us going.
—Don Byron, Oliver Ames High School basketball
coach, referring to one of his senior guards*

We jump-start a car when the battery has died. We give it a boost. Have you ever felt like you need a jump-start, a boost to get the day off on the right footing? Have you ever gone to bed, thinking about the next day and how you are going to "attack" the day, focus, be productive, and make it a great day?

What happens? The alarm goes off, and you press snooze one too many times. Now you're behind by ten to twenty minutes. The kids aren't cooperating in getting ready for school. Your outfit is wrinkled, or the shirt you were planning to wear is at the dry cleaner's. You finally get in the car to drive to your office or appointment and are stuck in traffic. You were so distracted by the morning at home you forgot about the new road construction starting today. You're tired and frustrated before you even begin your workday.

You have a presentation to prepare that needs to be ready by the end of the day. In looking at your smartphone when you're stopped at various traffic lights on the way to work, you see the e-mails that have been filling your inbox.

You arrive at work, and your manager enters your office with his cup of coffee and a pile of documents under his arm. The phone rings, and it's a very important client who needs updated information that only you can provide. You have a new employee who started earlier in the week, and you need to meet with her. Your administrative assistant comes into your office to let you know that you need to leave for a meeting now to meet with the company president. And on and on it goes. This is an average day for lots of people.

How can you jump-start your day so that you begin "on

track"? If you tend to get derailed before your day is really in full swing, begin by identifying what the causes may be. For example, if you are addicted to hitting the snooze button on your alarm clock, set the clock a little earlier. Even better, move it across the room so that you need to get up to turn it off.

Plan at the End of the Day

Is it better to plan your day at the end of the day or plan your day first thing in the morning? How you prepare for your day the day before will have the biggest impact on your daily production. Planning at the end of the day, when you are wrapping up your day, delivers an amazing return on that short amount of time you invest in it. I contend that you need five minutes or less.

When you plan at the end of the day, you've just "lived" your day, and it's still fresh in your head. Has someone ever asked you what you had for dinner the night before and you blank and can't remember? Then you know what can happen when you rely on your memory to piece together things you did the workday before on the morning after.

Maybe you've also had the experience of waking up in the middle of the night because you remembered something you need to add to your to-do list and then had to fumble around to write a note or send a text or e-mail to yourself. By putting closure to your day with a short planning session, you reduce the stress of remembering all the things that you feel you may have forgotten.

As you review the things on your task list that you haven't finished by the end of the day, you can move them to the day you plan to do them. Don't just move an undone task to the next day if there is no chance of getting to it. Be a thoughtful planner. If you don't move an incomplete task forward, you will constantly be playing catch-up and feeling like the undone tasks are piling up.

When we were in school, we learned number lines. Think about your tasks in this way: by not moving those items, they stay in the past and negative. Move them forward into the future, and they're positive.

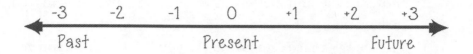

When you move your tasks, that's just the point: *you* move them. You continue to take charge of them by determining when you will work on them. If you leave them in the past, you constantly have to look backward. You feel behind, like you're constantly playing catch-up. You want to be looking forward. Taking that one step—cleaning your to-do list daily—allows you to be in charge. You are making the decisions about your day. Then you are ready the next day to get down to the work you want to do. No guessing, no trying to figure it out—you are ready.

The Boy Scout motto is "Be prepared." When you are prepared to start your day, knowing what you need to do, you will be more productive. If you wait to plan in the morning, the likelihood of getting distracted before you begin increases.

What are the things you can eliminate or adjust so that you can jump-start your day? Make a list of what you do in the morning. Is it spending too much time reading an online newspaper or getting on Facebook without a clear purpose? Do you spend more time talking to coworkers than you should? Do you get caught up in responding to e-mails that could wait?

Jump-start your day. Remove, as much as possible, the things that impact your ability to start your day focused on what needs to get done.

Next Steps

1. Give yourself five minutes to plan before you leave work or from wherever your workday is ending.
2. Move all the undone to-dos to another day that is more realistic to get them done.
3. List things that seem to derail your day before you've started and eliminate one of them. Just one at a time. When you're comfortable and consistent with eliminating one thing, move on to another one and just keep going.

K

Kaleidoscope

**Kaleidoscope: continually changing
pattern of shapes and colors; continually
shifting pattern, scene, and the like**

*Our days are a kaleidoscope. Every instant a change takes
place in the contents. New harmonies, new contrasts,
new combinations of every sort. Nothing ever happens
twice alike. The most familiar people stand each moment
in some new relation to each other, to their work, to
surrounding objects. The most tranquil house, with the most
serene inhabitants, living upon the utmost regularity of
system, is yet exemplifying infinite diversities.*
—*Henry Ward Beecher, American Congregationalist clergyman*

To this day, if I'm in a store and see a kaleidoscope, I am drawn to it. I can't resist the temptation to pick it up, put it to my eye, and see the various shapes that form as I turn the cylinder-shaped object. As I gaze, the patterns and colors change with just the slightest movement.

Our lives are very similar to a kaleidoscope. In an instant, they can be changed forever. In the preface, I shared with you stories of my mom and Stu's dad and a very difficult time in our lives. My mother suffered a head injury from a car accident that seemed to only break her ribs. Two months after the accident, she collapsed and was taken to the emergency room at our local hospital. Once there, she needed to be sent by ambulance to Brigham and Women's Hospital in Boston, where she had neurosurgery for a subdural hematoma. There were complications from the surgery that manifested themselves in a brain bleed.

Two and a half years later, after moving from the ICU to many-month-long hospital stays to rehabilitation facilities to skilled nursing facilities, she passed away two months after I was married. She wasn't able to attend the wedding. All of this turmoil was the result of what seemed to be a minor car accident. My family's life became a nightmare. We couldn't believe what our lives had become for those two and a half years.

In a moment, our lives were shattered. The way we lived each and every day was changed forever. I'm not sharing this story because I'm looking for pity or sympathy. I don't believe in pity parties for me or anyone else. My clients can attest to that. I was facing multiple challenges: wanting to emotionally support my father and family through this; dealing with insurance, estate planning, social workers, doctors, and other health-care providers; providing the best of myself to my clients in my two-year-old growing business; and being there for Stu, who was going through his own family crisis with the loss of his dad. My life was a kaleidoscope, only the cylinder wasn't turning slowly enough to enjoy the colorful beauty. The cylinder was spinning fast and seemed to be out of control.

What is point of this story?

Often we hear people reflect on life when a tragedy happens, such as losing a loved one. The longing to really appreciate life and live every day to its fullest is a commonly expressed theme. There isn't one person reading this book who hasn't experienced a sudden life-changing event. Whether it's a cancer diagnosis or a job loss or an accident or an unexpected bereavement, we have all experienced it.

Even if something is less tragic, like car problems or the school nurse asking us to come pick up a child who can't stop coughing, our life pattern shifts. Can we change the pattern of our day or someone else's day from a positive to a negative or from a negative to a positive?

Those of us who have children have experienced the patterns in our life changing daily. From infant to toddler to school-age to preteen to teen to young adult—life is in flux and constantly changing. Just as the kaleidoscope changes in an instant, so do our lives.

Using the kaleidoscope as a symbol, there are three areas that pertain to productivity to consider: the way we are affected by circumstances beyond our control, we are impacted by people's actions, and our actions impact others, both positively and negatively. Take a moment to ask yourself how each of these kaleidoscope shifts affects your life at home and at work.

How Do You Deal with Circumstances Beyond Your Control?

This is a question that can only be answered on a situation-by-situation basis. When faced with life-altering circumstances, removing the emotional component of your thinking may be difficult. Having the support of friends and family can make a difference.

Being prepared for something unfortunate may seem like a negative approach to life—or, if you are superstitious, you may believe that talking about something bad will cause it to happen. But the reality is that you want to make sure you have a plan in place, that your paperwork (living will, power of attorney, health-care proxy) and people to watch your kids or get into your house if necessary are all in place. Take that difficult step back to figure things out or have someone help you figure things out. Having your ducks in a row will allow you to better focus on the situation at hand.

How Do You React When You Are Impacted by Someone Else's Action?

Does someone cutting you off in traffic, a less-than-positive comment about your work, a difficult morning getting the kids off to school, or a call to "customer care" that makes you wonder if they really care set you off? There are so many ways that other people can influence our mood. Too often, we end up giving someone who doesn't deserve it too much power and influence over our day. We are trying to get something done, and we keep going back to that moment when somebody said something that irked us or put us in a bad mood, and we lose our ability to keep it together to do what needs to be done. As difficult as it can be, an important note to self is that if someone is able to have that much impact on us, then shame on us.

Take a step back and realize you have power and control over your actions and attitude. Breathe in and out to relax, and use self-talk to tell yourself you need to let it go. This individual isn't important enough to have this much influence over your life or even just this day. If you don't get back on track, it will cause a domino effect for the rest of the day or beyond.

How Do Your Actions Impact Others, Both Positively and Negatively?

The flipside of how others affect you is how you affect others. I like to think that in a very small way, we can influence someone else's day through random acts of kindness. This could be letting someone into traffic instead of cutting him or her off; holding a door open for someone; saying thank you; speaking in a kind and gentle manner when we could easily lose our temper; or simply smiling.

My son, Jonathan, and I were doing our monthly Sabbath service at a nursing home. Though this nursing home loved and cared for its residents, to me, it still seemed like a gloomy place. Jonathan and I were singing some of the prayers when I noticed that none of the residents was smiling. They all seemed sad. I made eye contact with one woman. I smiled at her. Her face lit up as she smiled back. Small gesture, big results.

During a delegating workshop I was conducting for an engineering firm, we were discussing the importance of feedback and appreciation. Out of the blue, one of the participants shared that a coworker had said something positive to him about the way he conducted himself while working on a project. It wasn't a manager but a peer. He felt terrific, and it gave him confidence in his abilities. Small, unexpected gesture, big results.

I chaired the rabbi search committee for my synagogue. When we decided that we weren't going to move forward with a rabbi candidate who we had interviewed via Skype or brought in for a face-to-face interview, I would call the candidate on the phone to convey the news. The difficulty of those phone calls was overwhelming, and many times I would cry after hanging up. However, I heard time and time again that the candidate appreciated hearing from me—instead of just receiving an e-mail or hearing nothing at all, which would have been easy options for me—and having the conversation. Obviously, they weren't happy with the results, but it helped them as they moved forward with their search.

When we become more aware of our surroundings and the little things we can do to make someone's life a little easier or happier, we should seize the opportunity. The unexpected result is that it makes us feel better, and feeling better is a good thing.

Next Steps

1. Are you ready for a personal crisis?
2. What do you need to do to prepare? What contingency planning should you do?
3. What is the first step to take?
4. What steps can you take to get back on track when something less crisis-driven gets to you?
5. What actions can you take that will positively impact people every day?

L

Lists

Lists: A series of names or other items written or printed together in a meaningful grouping or sequence so as to constitute a record; enumeration, schedule, line-up, to-dos

One of the secrets of getting more done is to make a To Do list every day, keep it visible, and use it as a guide to action as you go through the day.—Jean de la Fontaine, French poet

L ists can be an extraordinary way of helping you get organized. Lists can also be an extraordinary way of making you feel so overwhelmed that you don't get tasks done.

One client told me that he created several categories for his to-do lists. His topics included work tasks, home projects, career goals, and family. Each category required a to-do list; for example, he had a separate list for the home projects he wanted to tackle. The problem was that he didn't have a master list that included an action item to, for example, review the home projects list.

Let's examine two kinds of lists: short-term lists of things that need to be done almost immediately, and long-term lists of future items that we want to accomplish.

Short-Term To-Do List

The classic to-do list of tasks is, at best, the starting point for understanding what you need to do. Unfortunately, there are some downfalls to making this kind of list, including the following:

1. It doesn't include a deadline for completing a task.
2. To-do lists tend to multiply like rabbits; you begin making a list on a nice pad of paper and then the pad gets lost on the desk, and there's another pad of paper or scrap paper to add a to-do or two to the list.
3. The list tends to be rewritten and rewritten and rewritten, often with the same incomplete tasks needing to be done.
4. A to-do list can create such an overwhelming big picture,

like a wide-angle lens, that it becomes difficult to see how all the tasks *can* get done.

5. A long laundry list of actions that seems to never get whittled down can become an energy drain over time.

6. Creating a list of items you would like to do or work on that are in the future or put on the back burner easily slip through the cracks.

I've heard many clients say that they make a to-do list and never look at it, or they just choose the easy stuff to get done. I've also seen many people create a to-do list of "Today's To-Dos," only to look at the list and begin their day with an attitude of doom, telling themselves, "There's no way I can get to all of this. I'm not sure I can get even 25 percent of this accomplished." The day starts off on a negative note.

Beware of the Wish List

When I was leading a workshop many years ago, I had the participants begin planning their next five days by using sample planner pages. As I walked around the room, I noticed one gentleman's list had easily twenty-five items listed under "Today's Action List." I asked him if he thought it was realistic to get those things done that day, in light of attending a half-day offsite workshop and then having to drive back to his office. He replied with a resounding, "Yes!" He then qualified his answer, saying, "If I have no phone calls, no interruptions, and no e-mails, I should be able to do it all." When I then asked him if that scenario was realistic, he responded, "Not really."

The list he had created was a *wish list*. Wish lists are unrealistic for our purpose of getting things done. They end up distracting us from our priorities by adding things for the sake of crossing them off the list. They also distract us because what remains undone can weigh heavily on us. Consequently, getting things done becomes a matter of picking and choosing the "easy" things to accomplish—at the very least, to get them off the list. This may mean not having enough time to do the things that really are a priority.

Having too many lists with more lists on them isn't going to keep you focused on accomplishing the items you want. Maintaining too many lists can become just another daunting to-do on the to-do list.

Tune Your List

Like a musical instrument needs tuning, so does your approach to making your short-term to-do list. Be specific with the action you need to take. Use verbs to make an item action-oriented. Identify a specific day to work on it or do it.

An item on your to-do list like "Monthly Report" or "Basement," doesn't tell you what you need to do. It also doesn't help you determine how much time it may take you. Any items put on your to-do list should be in the form of an action. In other words, use verbs. For example, change "Basement" to "Go through three boxes in the basement—Feb. 12." Break "Monthly Report" down into multiple items, such as:

- E-mail contributors to the report asking for their data.—March 7
- Review data and begin inputting information into spreadsheet.—March 7
- Write overview and summary.—March 9

Include when you will do each item and enter it into the task list on your planner or calendar.

Your short-term to-do list should become a running list based on when you will work on things. It's not something that you should have to recreate each day or week; instead, you are constantly updating it as new to-dos come your way. This is also why, when making your list, the priority items may not always be at the top of the list. You may be entering something onto your list that you won't work on until a week from Monday. As your current week continues, you will probably be adding things to do on that Monday. When Monday rolls around, what you put in a week earlier may be less important than you originally thought.

Long-Term To-Do List

A client asked, "What do I do with a to-do that I don't really need to do now but want to act on sometime in the future?" In this particular case, it was changing her car insurance. We all have things we need to or want to get done, but there's no sense of urgency or immediacy. How can you prevent them from being put so far back on the back burner that they end up falling off the stove and slipping through the proverbial cracks?

One strategy is to put an action into the task list on your planner or calendar (electronic or paper) to review whatever the item is at a time that works better for you or when it makes more sense to revisit the item. In the case of the car insurance, my client took on two action items instantly: checking to see when the renewal comes up and determining when she needed to begin researching new insurance so that the renewal date didn't come and go, leaving her stuck with the same insurance for another year.

If there is a time or date when you need to complete a long-term to do, work backward from that date to figure out when you need to start doing something about it. Remember that the more you can put on active lists that you keep current and that you use, the less you need to keep in your head. Trying to remember things when they're not written down adds unnecessary stress to your life, and this is something over which you do have control.

Next Steps

1. Make your to-do list specific, using action words (breaking things down).
2. Put your actions into the task list on your planner or calendar.

3. For a long-term item on a long-term to-do list, put a reminder into your planner or calendar to revisit the item. And if the timing is still not right when you revisit it, put a reminder into your planner for a future date to revisit it again.

M

Maxed Out

**Maxed out: to reach or cause to reach
the full extent or allowance**

*A schedule so tight that it would only work if I didn't sleep
on Monday nights. —Alan Jay Lerner, lyricist and librettist*

Calendars fill up with meetings, deadlines, presentations, errands, laundry, grocery shopping, buying gifts and cards, and projects at work and home—not to mention picking up and dropping off children from after-school activities while homework and school projects need to get done. Our calendars are like a balloon that we try to get bigger and bigger until—you, guessed it—*boom!* It explodes.

The solution is to *not* max out your schedule so that there is very little time to breathe or room for error. Unfortunately, so many of us do the opposite—we try to cram so much into whatever time we think is available that we are bound to drop something.

"MAXED OUT!"

september

3 4 5

18

1. Rent Duel

9 Lunch at 2

12. Dr.s

At Work

I was working with a client who had a wish list of things she wanted to get done "today." When I asked her to figure out how much time it would take her to do each item—even being idealistic—she saw that when she added it all up, she would have had to stay at work until two a.m. I asked her if that was what she had planned. Her response was, of course, no.

Take charge of your schedule and take a step back to really understand the implications of maxing out. It can be eye-opening.

Do you double-book yourself into two meetings at the same time or have to leave one meeting early to get to another meeting late? What message are you sending to others? What type of stress are you putting on yourself? Are you distracted in each of the meetings because you can't be fully present? Do you overbook yourself when you travel because you "have no choice"—you are at your company's office in another state or country, and you have to see everyone?

Be honest with yourself. Do you have control over events? Are you sure that others are causing you to max out your schedule? Author and psychotherapist Stephen C. Paul says, "You don't get to control any outcome, only every choice you make along the way." When something comes up that you need to enter into your calendar, do you check your schedule to see what else is going on around that time?

How can you refrain from maxing out your time? The first thing to do is to acknowledge that maxing out your schedule isn't working for you. By leaving unscheduled time in your schedule, you increase your flexibility to deal with the unexpected or to fully be present.

At Home

At work, a maxed-out schedule has a lot to do with choices we make. At home, it's also about choices, and dealing with the choices you've made. With an increase of scheduled and unscheduled activities, it's critical to maintain a family tracking system to record who has to be where, who's dropping off whom, and who's doing pickup. Schedules need to be coordinated and communicated. Contingencies also need to be put into place for the unexpected and spontaneous. For example, do you have a designated someone you can contact to help you if you are stuck in traffic and will be late to pick up your youngster?

When the schedule becomes maxed out, meaning there is little time to breathe or for any kind of unexpected mishap to occur, stress and confusion increases.

A mom with four children declares at the start of the school year, "Let the stress begin!" Is this the way to start a school year? When children are overscheduled, parents are overscheduled. Running around from one activity to another takes its toll on the entire family. Even the child who is not in school yet and too young for extracurricular activities is being carted from one drop-off location to another pickup location and back and forth and forth and back. The following can result when you drain your energy pool with maxed-out schedules:

- Kids are too tired to do homework.
- Parents are too tired to help with homework.
- Parents are too worn-out to "be in the moment" and just enjoy the evening.
- Things to do and places to be are forgotten.
- Someone is always rushing from activity to activity
- Intrafamily communication is put on the perpetual back burner.

Managing the calendar to avoid maxing it out is essential to keeping chaos in check. When you fail to take a good hard look at what is being scheduled, you cost yourself and everyone else time and stress.

You may be thinking, "I can squeeze in one more activity or to-do because my son really needs to be exposed to lacrosse, even though he's already playing basketball and taking violin twice a week. My daughter only has dance, piano, and tennis.

I can make it fit. It will be difficult, but I can do it." But ask the hard questions: Are you maxing out your calendar? Are you maxing out your children's calendars? Do you and your family have the time capacity to handle the schedule you've created? When you overextend yourself or others, stress and anxiety rule the day. Take the following six steps to go from maxed out to manageable:

1. Examine your list of family activities (include those that are scheduled and those that you would like to be doing).

2. Estimate the amount of time each takes up; this includes commuting back and forth in addition to the time spent at the activity. Don't subtract time for carpooling. Assume that your family is going solo.

3. Justify the need for the activity or activities.

4. Prioritize the list.

5. Determine if any items can or should be removed, now or at a future date—meaning that if you are in the middle of Little League baseball season and your son is committed to a team, canceling the activity may be an option but it's not the best solution at this time.

6. Look at your schedule in your personal planner or calendar and the family calendar. Pencil in any information you know about scheduled activities. Go out as far into the future for which you have information. Block out the necessary amount of time the activity requires.

What do you see? Is the schedule doable without draining your family's energy? Can you see overlaps or potential problems? Addressing potential struggles now will save you time, energy, and sanity down the road.

Next Steps

At Work

1. Take an eye-opening look at your work schedule for the next few weeks.
2. Where do you see your schedule being maxed out?
3. Make realistic and helpful adjustments.

The further out you look, the easier it is to change things. It is much more difficult to reschedule things that are happening tomorrow.

At Home

1. Make a list of all family activities, including those you would like to be doing. Estimate the amount of time they take, including round-trip commuting as well as time for the activity.
2. Using a calendar, map out the schedule of activities. Look at the calendar and use your ability to anticipate. Is the schedule doable, or is it going to create undue stress? Prioritize the list of activities (for yourself and your children) and determine what activity or activities can and should be removed.
3. Regularly sit down with your children and go over their daily assignments and projects. Help them get in the habit of effectively using their assignment book or planning tool. You are showing support by discussing how they can accomplish what they need to do. Break things down into small, bite-size, doable tasks and schedule them into their planner.

Not only will you better understand their assignments, deadlines, and possible obstacles to completing schoolwork, but you will start to see the importance of calendar maintenance and reducing maxed-out schedules, theirs and yours.

N

No

No: an expression of dissent, denial, or refusal, as in response to a question

And it comes from saying no to 1,000 things to make sure we don't get on the wrong track or try to do too much. We're always thinking about new markets we could enter, but it's only by saying no that you can concentrate on the things that are really important.
—Steve Jobs, American entrepreneur and inventor

One of the smallest words in the dictionary, when used effectively, is one of the most powerful ways of transforming chaos into calm. Being confident and willing to say no is vital. The common, knee-jerk reaction I've seen working with my clients is that, when asked to do something, they say, "Sure, yes, give it to me, I'll get it done."

There are many reasons to say yes, which we'll explore when we get to the chapter on "Yes." And there are an equal number of reasons to say no. Common reasons for not saying no include, but aren't limited to, the following:

- fear of not being seen as a team player
- desire to be perceived as the hero, problem-solver, and go-to person
- lack of a clear idea of preexisting time commitments
- guilt
- fear of losing one's job

Do You Want to Say Yes or No?

One of the best and easiest ways to figure this out is to think first before you commit. You're on the phone with or you've received an e-mail from someone asking you to participate on a committee or task force or take a leadership role in a community event. You hang up the phone or press *send* in response to the e-mail with an affirmative response. Now, how do you feel? Are you wondering what you just did or asking yourself why you said yes? Are you dreading getting involved?

Before you say *yes*, imagine how you will feel after you've said it. If your intuition and gut are saying, *No, don't do it*, you would be wise to say no or look for ways to say a positive no. But don't just rely on your gut—look at your commitments. Does it make sense to take on something in addition to other obligations?

A Positive No

One of the easiest ways to overcome any reluctance to saying no is to do it positively. Offering a positive no doesn't mean going up to someone who has asked you to do something, grinning at them, and playfully or sarcastically saying, "No!" A positive no allows you to offer ways to be helpful and involved without making a commitment that you really don't want to or are unable to make. Here are some ways to articulate a positive no:

- Ask questions to show your sincere interest in learning more.
- Provide a resource, someone with comparable knowledge or more knowledge.
- Offer to get someone else.
- Give the individual necessary information so that he or she can move forward on his or her own.
- Explain your schedule and offer alternative times for your involvement.
- Ask if it really needs to be done *now*.
- If the person is circumventing proper channels to involve you in something, explain the proper channels and rules for gaining the information.
- Schedule a meeting to discuss the situation.
- Offer to work on part of the project or to complete a portion of it, but not the entire body of work.

Actually Saying No

If you find it easy to say no, then you are all set. But if you have difficulty mustering up the courage you need to say no, realize that you can do it. When you are asked to do something and you aren't sure you want to do it or you want to think about it first or you *know* you don't want to do it but are reluctant to say no, tell the person you need to get back to him or her and be specific as to when you will have an answer.

Prepare what you are going to say. Practice in your head or aloud. If you aren't prepared, you will stammer, hem, and haw, and then potentially get wrangled into a commitment. Having a conversation may be more difficult, but it's polite and direct. There are no mixed messages or intentions that are misunderstood in a text or e-mail. Remember, the best way to approach the conversation is with a positive no. For example, you might say something like the following:

Hi, Nancy. Thank you for asking me to participate on this important committee. The work sounds fascinating, and it's a great opportunity for those involved. Unfortunately, at this time, my schedule doesn't permit me to work on it. I hope you will keep me in mind in the future.

There are some key things not to say when you are saying no:

- Don't make excuses. When you start going into all your troubles and woes, you turn your positive no into something very negative.
- Don't tell someone that you "just don't have the time." The reality is, no one has the time, but some people choose how they will commit their time, and it may be differently from how you would commit your time.

Stu (my husband) and I have been active in our synagogue for many years. Stu has been treasurer for several years, and I have been a vice president and chaired many committees, including the religious school and rabbi search. We are very purposeful about why we do what we do, and we know that our commitments are quite time-consuming. But because we have our reasons, we do them. We may not always be smiling about it, but we do them.

As part of my responsibility as chair of the religious school committee, I needed to telephone our families to ask them to attend an event. During one of my conversations with a dad, I was taken aback by his comments to me. He didn't want to attend the event. As we were conversing, he said that he couldn't believe how active my husband and I were in the temple. He said, "I can't do it. I don't have the time."

I retorted, rather indignantly, "We don't have the time either, but we make the time."

I should have commended him for his honesty and ability to say no. However, I was annoyed by the way he said it. My point is that you need to be careful how you come across when you are saying no. After my ruffled feathers smoothed out, I realized that he had different priorities that worked for him and his family. He probably had no clue as to how he sounded to someone who does work hard for an organization and takes time away from other things because it *is* a priority.

Saying no can be quite powerful. Use your power wisely. The more clear your priorities are to you—whether it's family, friends, health, community, or work—the more focused you will be and the easier it will be to know when to say no or yes. If a potential commitment doesn't fit into your priorities, then you need to truly weigh the consequences of saying yes and the benefits of saying no.

Every time you say yes to something, you are potentially saying no to something to which you already said yes. Think about it.

Next Steps

1. Think about a time when you said yes to something and wished you had said no.
2. How could you have handled it differently?
3. Think about upcoming possibilities. What do you want to say no to?
4. Work out a strategy for saying no positively.

O

One Last Thing

One last thing: a single final action

I just got one last thing, I urge all of you, all of you, to enjoy your life, the precious moments you have. To spend each day with some laughter and some thought, to get your emotions going. —Jim Valvano, American college basketball coach

I f you take Jim Valvano's advice, then you are all set. Mr. Valvano's urging is the goal of this chapter as well as the message of *It's About Time!*

I wish this chapter was really about that "one last thing," but it isn't. That's because there will almost always be one last thing to do. Determining whether it's necessary to do that one last thing or you can leave something undone can be a difficult decision. Through the years, many clients have said, in some way or another, that it's hard to stop working at the end of the day when they still have so much more they could do. The irony is, if everything does get done and there is no more to do, then you probably won't have a job for long.

Being able to stop, whether at work or at home, is a necessary skill that involves setting boundaries. The boundaries aren't those you set for others to follow to guard your time; they are the boundaries you create for yourself. Be tough on yourself about adhering to your boundaries. Give yourself permission to stop, be it at work or at home. Acknowledge all you've accomplished and that it's time to be done.

Here's my theory as to why we find this so difficult to do. Throughout academic life, from the time we were in elementary school and up through college, the school year was neatly packaged. Papers were written and turned in, tests were taken, homework was completed, desks were cleaned out, lockers were emptied, and we were *done*. It was a complete sense of accomplishment, with no residual action. This was life through our childhood and teens, and maybe even into young adulthood.

That sense of being done was one that may have carried over

to a summer job as well. Once the job was over, it was back to school. There was nothing to add to the to-do list.

Enter the real world. Each day brings more actions and projects that are, of necessity, going to have to be left incomplete in the short term. This may create a sense of discomfort.

Peter's Successful Choice

One of my clients, Peter, had the best of intentions about getting home in time to eat dinner with his family. Unfortunately, Peter would see, as the end of the workday neared, an overloaded, unrealistic to-do list with many incomplete items. He would ask me, "What's the big deal if I send one more e-mail?" In answering his own question, he admitted that sending one more e-mail meant that he would see additional e-mails that were recently sent to him and feel compelled to respond. At the same time, every e-mail sent or responded to meant one more thing checked off the list and one less thing to do the next day.

Peter had two unsatisfactory options if he wanted to continue at this pace:

1. He could keep staying late at work to finish up. Unfortunately, the result was missing family meals quite regularly.
2. He could do work from home after his children went to bed. Unfortunately this choice would cut into the time he wanted to spend with his wife.

Instead, Peter chose to plan the end of his day better by doing the following:

- He predetermined what time he wanted to leave.
- He entered "wrapping up the day," with a few specific action items (like reading e-mail), into his schedule.

- He left himself enough time to do the last end-of-the day items based on the day, his workload, and his pace at responding to e-mails.
- He set an alarm on his computer and cell phone for twenty to thirty minutes prior to the time he wanted to leave as a reminder that he had a specific amount of time left in his workday.
- He made up his mind to adhere to his plan and leave.

Do you have an end-of-the-day routine? What steps can you take to avoid "one last thing"?

Next Steps

1. Identify the "one last things" you do.
2. Identify where in your schedule, toward the end of the day, you can fit them.
3. Determine when you want to stop each day. Work backward from that time to figure out what time you need to begin your end-of-the-day routine. Every day may be different, but taking a few moments at the beginning of your day to figure it out helps minimize time spent doing "one last thing" and encountering unwanted results.

Bonus O

Options

Options: alternatives; choices; the act of choosing

Strategic planning will help you fully uncover your available options, set priorities for them, and define the methods to achieve them.—Robert J. Mckain, American author

When issues and problems arise, our first reaction tends to be a search for a quick resolution. Another reaction is to simply stop focusing, get caught up in the problem, let it spin out of control, and shut down.

A better alternative is to stop and weigh the available options. Looking at a problem and thinking through viable routes for getting it solved will make the difference in how much time and energy you save or lose.

A few months before my son was going to enter kindergarten, I thought his after-school schedule was all set until I received a call from the after-school program for which he was registered. The director said that the schedule I submitted—Tuesdays, Wednesdays, and Thursdays (my choice for my full days of work)—wasn't available. Instead, he could go Monday, Tuesday, and Friday, or I could change him from morning kindergarten to the afternoon session and have him bused three times during the day before I picked him up. The options presented to me were unacceptable.

I got off the phone and cried.

After my momentary pity party (I don't believe in pity parties, not even for myself), I talked to myself, asking, *Mitzi, what are your options? What are some alternative solutions?* I proceeded to do some research on available after-school programs, made some phone calls, scheduled some appointments to visit places, and, after a few days, came up with a solution that was even better than my original plan.

When I laid out the options, developed my plan to resolve the issue, and then started taking positive steps to resolve it, I felt I was back in control. Though my stress didn't go away completely, it became a minor annoyance. Being in the driver's seat, so to speak, was all I needed.

The point of writing out options is to allow choices to manifest and be made in a methodical way. Take the possible emotional component out of the equation by putting the options in front of you and thinking them through. If what you decide turns into an emotional decision, so be it—but have the information you need to make an informed decision.

Next Steps

1. Once you realize that you can weigh your options, clear your head by using the method that works best for you—for example, breathing deeply, walking around, or listening to music.
2. Write down your available options.
3. Take a good look at the list.
4. Decide what is most important to you in determining which option you choose.
5. Ask yourself, "Do I need to talk to anyone or get any additional information before I choose an option, or is getting more information part of the steps I need to take before I make a choice?"

P

Perception

Perception: a specific idea, concept, impression formed

Perception is reality.—Lee Atwater,
American political consultant

Here is a key factor to interacting successfully with people: their perceptions are their reality, whether it's someone else's perception of you or your own perception of yourself. The message you convey and the image you create is what will distinguish you from others. Your image of a well put-together individual who isn't easily flustered, meets deadlines, and gets the job done will work wonders for you, both in terms of your career and your personal life. Your image is what people see, and that includes your actions. Your actions directly impact your reliability and credibility. They establish how people treat you.

A person's image can easily become tarnished by missed deadlines, unreturned phone calls, e-mails not responded to in a timely manner, or an appearance of being harried and out of control. You make excuses, a lot of excuses, and most of the time, the excuse is that you're "very busy." Is this busy image helping or hurting you?

You want to be seen as someone who is organized, works hard, meets goals, and gets things done, without making it seem as though you are stressed or a martyr, constantly suffering and making sure others know about it. You can project this image by taking some simple steps.

Think of the phrase "dress for success." The expression conjures up a put-together person from head-to-toe, confident and self-assured. Just as you would dress for success, you can organize for success and have the same kind of confident, put-together image.

Can you fake it? To a degree you can—maybe fake it until you make it. Even the most disorganized person can send a message that says, "I am organized," even if it's only an illusion.

An organized image not only helps you become more organized and work more efficiently, but it can open wonderful doors of possibility as well.

"What image do you want to project?"

Let's look at some specific situations.

Deadlines

Know what's on your plate. When you are asked to do something, provide managers, customers/clients, and coworkers with a realistic expectation of what you can do. Nothing destroys credibility more than overpromising and under-delivering. When people question whether they can rely on you to get a job done, your reputation suffers and your ability to advance will, at some point, be negatively impacted. It could be during your performance review, discussions of increasing your salary, or pursuit of available promotions. When you can confidently communicate your workload and any obstacles that you foresee in meeting a deadline, you enhance your image.

Communicate potential problems with meeting deadlines in advance. Do it effectively and with conviction. One of my clients, a bank president, told me that he would much prefer to have someone give him advance warning that a deadline might be missed than to not know where something stood and not have it delivered on time without any warning or explanation.

Procrastination

Procrastination will set you back. It drains your mental energy and time. You engage in other activities you don't need to do in order to avoid doing what you need to do. Even though you are putting something off, it's still there, right in front of you, waiting to be done. Try the following tips for preventing procrastination:

- Determine why you are procrastinating. Is there a valid reason, or are you just putting off the inevitable and causing yourself and others stress and headaches?
- Get and/or have all the information you need to proceed.
- Break things down into small, bite-size, doable pieces.
- Work with someone who will keep you accountable.
- Reward yourself after completing key milestones.
- Uncover the worst thing that can happen if you start working on it.
- Make up your mind to just do it!

Workspace

Walk into your space as though you are a visitor, seeing it for the first time. What do you notice first? Sit in the visitor's seat or create a place for a visitor to sit. What does that individual see? Could he or she be distracted by the clutter or disorganization? That's where you want to begin.

Clear shelves of random paper and straighten out binders, books, and catalogs. If your desk surface is covered with spread-out papers, be aware that this method doesn't help your image. At least make small, neat piles. Don't have a blotter or blotter calendar on your desk. It just looks like more paper. You want as much of your desk surface to show as possible. Nothing should be put on the floor—for example, no shoes, umbrellas, clothing, or piles of work. Get bins and put your belongings in them.

If you are serious about cleaning up and not just about creating an organized image, write down your system before you begin. Think of your papers as categories of information. Try the following tips:

- Schedule time, regularly, to clean up and throw things away.
- Have supplies handy, such as hanging files, folders, and labels.
- Put papers in their "home" files so you can avoid using tiered file holders on surface areas.
- Put mugs and mugs holding pencils and pens away.
- Keep only what you use regularly on the surface. For example, if you don't use scotch tape regularly, put it in a drawer.
- Don't let your inbox or outbox overflow. Go through them regularly.

Speaking with Others

You may think that telling people how busy you are sends a positive message—that you are invaluable to an organization. Think again.

Ask yourself, *What is the message I send to others when I tell them how busy I am and that I am busy all the time?* If you want new business, telling potential or existing clients how busy you are makes them question your ability to focus on their needs. I had a friend to whom I could easily have referred some business, but I chose someone else because my friend was always "so busy." I didn't think she could take on any additional work.

When you speak fast and rush through conversations, the message you are sending is that you don't have time to talk. This may be the message you want to send, but be careful to whom you are doing this. Be aware.

You may think that being busy and letting people know how hard you work is helping your image, but managers want to see people get their work done and make it appear effortless. Complaining or telling war stories about how hard you work or how late you stayed doesn't contribute to that impression. I have had many a client wonder why a member of the team can't get work done during *regular* business hours and needs to stay so late, so often. Your coworkers may wonder how efficient and effective your performance is instead of appreciating your commitment.

Acting flustered or absentminded while talking to others does not send a message of professionalism. If, for example, you are on the phone with a client and can't find a document under discussion, don't pretend you have the document and try to fake it. Stop the conversation and say, "Let me look for it and get back to you in just a moment. I want to have that information in front of me, and it will take me a moment to find it. I don't want to waste your time while I'm looking for it." Sound calm and focused.

The following tips about speaking with others may also be helpful:

- Do deep breathing as a regular exercise to help you when speaking, especially if you are anxious and nervous.

- Don't come across as defensive.
- Don't make excuses.
- Saying "I'm sorry" puts you in a negative position unless you have done something that actually warrants an apology.

Meetings

*I have noticed that the people who are late
are often so much jollier than the people who
have to wait for them.—E. V. Lucas*

It's very easy to positively or negatively impact your image when it comes to meetings. Obey the following rules to make sure you're on the positive side:

- Arrive on time! If you're late, don't call attention to your tardiness. Apologize quietly and sit down. If you know in advance that you will be late, let the person who is running the meeting know.
- Arrive prepared. Prior to the meeting, read materials that you know will be discussed. Don't try to fake it by reviewing materials as you are trying to discuss them.
- Prepare key points that you would like to make.
- Speak in bullet points. Be clear and concise. Don't ramble or tell stories that get the meeting off track.
- Don't contribute to making the meeting get off track. Think first, think twice, and then speak. Be relevant.
- Be cognizant of what you physically take into meetings: bags, paperwork, computers, smartphones, tablets, devices, and files. They project an image. Do you look neat? Do your accoutrements look put together? Do you end up spreading your stuff out and taking up too much

space? Does your gear look organized? Can you find what you need? Pencil? Pen? Paper? Tablet?

- Does your phone go off? Are you so distracted by your technology that you distract others or appear to be rude? Don't answer the phone when you are in a meeting, even in a one-on-one or small group. Answering a call during a meeting sends the message that your meeting isn't important. If you are expecting a call that you need to take, be up front about that at the start of your meeting.

E-mails and Phone Calls

You can use e-mails, texts, and phone calls to help create positive perceptions. The following rules will help you make that good impression:

- Return phone calls and e-mails in a timely fashion.
- Be prepared for phone calls and conference calls; have materials you need available.
- Make phone calls or send e-mails to people you are supposed to get back to, even if it's only to tell them that you don't have anything to tell them and that you are continuing to work on their project.
- Carefully read any e-mails you are sending to make sure there aren't any grammar or spelling errors.
- Get to the point.
- Make the subject line as specific as possible.
- Update your outgoing voice mail message daily. This may seem like a waste of time, but it makes you appear current and on-the-job.

Briefcases and Computer Bags

What kind of first impression do you make when you walk

into a room? Do you look like a "bag person," ready to drop from the weight of what you are carrying? Can you find what you are looking for in your computer bag, such as connectors and battery packs? Can you find all the necessary papers because your briefcase is organized, with labeled file folders and information that is easy to retrieve? The following are some tips for organizing these useful carriers:

- Clean out what you carry around with you (briefcase, computer bag, pocketbook, wallet), including anything that you will use in front of other people.
- Use folders and label them.
- Practice pulling out information. Imagine what someone in a meeting may ask for and practice taking it out. Are you fumbling, or are you prepared and agile?
- Before you leave work to go home, make sure you have what you need for the next day.
- Look at yourself in a full-length mirror to see what other people see when you are carrying your accessories.
- Don't carry hanging folders around. They get caught on things and look unprofessional. Leave them in the drawers.

As a general rule, carry your calendar, planner, or schedule (including task list) with you. That way, when someone asks you to do something or schedule something, you are prepared. Creating the perception of being organized can be quite simple. The biggest challenge is being consistent. Once you see the payback, your determination will keep you moving forward.

Your self-image, knowing you can get things done with ease, goes hand-in-hand with your credibility. Your company, clients, family, and friends will feel confident in you. More importantly, you will feel confident in yourself. You will reduce your stress and anxiety and the stress of those around you.

Next Steps

1. Determine what kind of image you project, either by being honest with yourself or asking someone you trust.
2. What area or areas do you need to work on? Write down one or two actions you can take to change your image and organize for success.

Q

Quality Time

Quality time: time devoted exclusively to nurturing a cherished person or activity

Your children can be around you all day, but if you don't spend quality time with them and you don't pay attention to them and talk to them and listen to them, it doesn't matter that they're just around you.
—Brandy Norwood, American recording artist

When you hear the term *quality time,* what comes to mind? Do you think about spending more time with a particular person, be it a child, spouse, partner, friend, relative, or coworker? Does having more time to do things that you want to do come to mind?

My guess would be that the former is more likely to be your answer and that the latter may not have occurred to you. In this chapter, I will share with you ways to get quality time however you define it, whether it's time for yourself or time you want to spend with others.

To begin, it's necessary for you to define quality time. If you can't define it, you're going to have difficulty creating it. Quality time can be whatever you want it to be. It can be time for yourself or time you spend with others or a combination of both. However, you must decide what it is at this moment in your life. Because our lives are fluid, it will change over time, and it will keep changing. With change, you will need to reevaluate what is important to you.

If you are being pulled in too many directions by too many people with too many demands, it's time to weed out what you shouldn't be doing and look at ways to lessen those burdens. They'll drain you of energy and make it difficult for you to schedule quality time.

Defining Your Rocks

In my workshop "Balance? Juggle? Find Time for You!" I share a story that originates from Dr. Stephen Covey's book *First Things First.* This is the version I share in my program. Even if you've heard similar versions or seen his demonstration, it's worth looking at again.

A professor wanted to teach his class a lesson on time management. To begin his lesson, he placed a large fishbowl on his desk and put several large rocks in it until they reached the top of the bowl. He asked the students if the fishbowl was full. They answered yes, it was indeed full.

The professor then took a container of small pebbles and poured them into the bowl. The pebbles filtered into the empty spaces between the large rocks. After the pebbles had settled, he asked his class again if the bowl was full.

By now they had caught on and told him that it wasn't full. He smiled and then brought out a container of sand and poured the sand into the bowl. The grains of sand trickled in between the rocks and the pebbles. After the container was empty, he again asked his class if the bowl was full. Again the response was no, it wasn't full.

The professor pulled out a container filled with water. He poured the water into the fishbowl until it was filled right to the top. He asked his class if the fishbowl was full. This time the class responded with a resounding yes! The professor then asked, "What's the lesson?"

One student raised his hand eagerly to reply. He said that no matter what you have going on, you can keep adding more.

The profession responded that no, that wasn't the lesson. The lesson is that if you don't put your big rocks in first, there's a greater chance you won't get them in at all.

What are the five most important "big rocks" currently in your life? Are you able to define your life's priorities and narrow them down to five? Take some time to reflect upon this. Think about the story and then put those rocks in your jar first. Can you put yourself at the top of the list?

During one of my coaching sessions, I told this story to my

client, a bank president. We discussed it, and at the end of the meeting we scheduled my next appointment to see him. A few weeks passed before I returned to his office. While we were talking, my eye caught sight of a rock on his desk. I asked him why it was there. He picked it up and showed me that the front was painted and had writing on it. He explained that he and his family went on vacation, and he shared the "big rocks" story. His family, intrigued by the idea, found a good-size rock and decided to paint the front. My client was charged with writing out his three big rocks on the painted rock.

What Are YOUR Big Rocks?

This is what he wrote:
1. Myself (health)
2. My family
3. Work

I asked him why he put himself first (which I thought was fabulous). He explained that if he didn't have his health, then he wouldn't be there for his family. My client decided to take care of himself first and foremost and spend quality time exercising and looking for pockets of time to do it.

Being clear on your priorities will help you say yes or no to things that either help you stay focused on your big rocks or divert you from them. Saying yes must be based on your priorities. If one of your priorities is to spend more time with your children and you are asked to be on a committee at school, saying yes may look like you are doing something for your children, but you're not doing something *with* your children.

You have choices in how you live your life, how you react to situations, and how you self-manage.

Time and Energy Drains

There are things in our lives that drain our time and energy. Identifying what they are and getting rid of them helps make room for other things—those things that you want to enter your life. As inventor Alexander Graham Bell said, "When one door closes, another opens; but we often look so long and so regretfully upon the closed door that we do not see the one which has opened for us."

My client June lost her husband, leaving her to raise a young son alone. During one of our coaching sessions, June told me that she was sad. Her son, now a teenager, shut himself in his bedroom when she came home from work. When she asked him why, he explained that as soon as she walked in the door, the house felt chaotic. She didn't know what to do. She wanted her house to be a pleasant and calm place for her son, not the opposite.

My conversation with June went something like this:

Mitzi: What do you do when you get home from work?

June: I say hi to my son, turn the TV on, and start getting dinner ready. While dinner is cooking, I usually iron work clothes for the next day.

Mitzi: Why do you turn the TV on as soon as you get home?

June: The news is on, and I have to find out tomorrow's weather.

Mitzi: You may not realize this, but the TV makes instant noise, and this could be creating the feeling of commotion. There is a phone number you can call to get the weather for the next day. I'll write it down for you. [*When I was working with June, it wasn't commonplace to have a home computer or laptop. Going to www.weather.com or any other website wasn't an option.*] Here are two suggestions. One, when you walk in the door, leave the TV off. Two, schedule your ironing so that you are doing it only once or twice a week. Let's see if you and your son notice a different dynamic.

Sure enough, the next time we met, she told me that she left the TV off, eliminating the noise, and reworked her ironing schedule. When she gets home, she and her son greet each other. Her son does his homework at the kitchen table while June prepares dinner. This gives them time to talk and be together.

June eliminated an energy drain by tweaking one small thing: keeping the TV off. However, the impact made a huge difference in the quality of their time and their quality time with each other.

In one of my workshops, when we were discussing time and energy drains, a participant said that she had a mole on her back and should make a doctor's appointment to check it out. She was quite worried about it, and it was becoming more and more of a daily distraction. But she was concerned about what the doctor would find and put off scheduling an appointment. Her action item from the workshop was to make that appointment.

A few weeks later, she called me and told me that the mole was nothing. She was now able to focus on a rock with more energy and gusto, knowing that she was healthy. What is draining you—relationships (friends or family needing too much from you, wanting to break up with your girlfriend/boyfriend), finances (big bills or not paying your bills on time, causing financial difficulties), work, your home (possibly in need of repairs or updating), your health (overweight, not eating healthy)? Are there things you can delegate, or can you better manage expectations?

Once you begin to remove these obstacles, you will have more time for quality time. The message of *It's About Time!* continues to be about planning and taking action. To get the quality time you desire, you must take the steps to get you there. The quality time you desire may not manifest itself in mega hours but in special moments when you can truly be present with yourself and for yourself, or with other people.

Before you begin your quest for quality time, keep in mind that if you decide that the quality time is for you, you aren't being selfish. It's a way for you to reinvigorate and reenergize *you*! If you aren't able to find the time for *you*, you may become resentful or grumpy or worse. If that happens, you aren't helping anyone, at work or home.

Guilt is wasted energy, unless you have done something truly wrong. Guilt can cause resentment.

Next Steps

1. Write out a sentence or phrase that defines quality time for you (what you will do with it and who you will spend it with—even if it's just you).
2. Define your rocks. Limit yourself to five to keep the list

focused. It may not be easy to limit the number to five, but it will help you keep from getting distracted.

3. Define your time and energy drains. What is an action you can take to begin eliminating one? Just start with one.

4. What is the first action you can take to begin adding more time in your calendar for your rocks?

R

Routine

Routine: commonplace tasks, chores, or duties that must be done regularly or at specified intervals; typical or everyday activity

All of us, from time to time, need a plunge into freedom and novelty, after which routine and discipline will seem delightful by contrast.—Andre Maurois, French author

Several years ago, I watched my son, as I did every morning, enter his kindergarten classroom. I waited by the window because he always came over and waved good-bye. It was our way, our ritual; however, on this one morning I observed him more closely.

His teacher had established a routine for all the children to follow. First, they turned in their communications folders; second, they put their snack in their cubby; and third, they hung up their backpacks and jackets. This was just one part of my son's ritual in a routine-filled day.

For children, there is a sense of comfort and safety in knowing what to expect on a daily basis. As adults, we set up our routines, even the simple task of brushing our teeth. Before brushing, we first take our toothbrush and put toothpaste and water on it. As elementary as this routine is, it demonstrates how certain rituals allow us to not think about what to do next. They become mindless habits.

Think about how unsettling deviating from the norm is for you. Changes such as moving to a new town, starting a new job, entering a new school, starting a school year, getting married or divorced, or suddenly caring for a sick relative or friend can be disruptive. Even changes like construction altering the route to and from work, new responsibilities added to your job, reorganization in your company, working with a new manager, or policy changes that affect the current processes can increase your stress.

When we establish daily, weekly, or monthly routines or rituals, we can begin to see a reduction in stress as comfort begins to emerge. Those who resist routine commonly refer to routine as being "in a rut" or lacking spontaneity. In their book *The Power of Full Engagement,* authors Jim Loehr and Tony Schwartz argue that "far from precluding spontaneity, rituals provide a level of comfort, continuity and security that free us to improvise and to take risks. Rituals provide a stable framework in which creative breakthroughs often occur."

My client Harold meets with the president of his company biweekly to review his work and discuss current department and industry issues. Harold doesn't necessarily relish the meeting preparation, but he knows this is a regularly scheduled event. He is ready, and the meetings are productive.

Jane, a recruiter for a bank, works for a manager who thinks nothing of calling a department meeting on a whim. The manager's expectation is that all her direct reports will stop whatever they are working on and attend her meeting. The result for Jane is cancelling already scheduled appointments with job candidates (even as they sit in the lobby) and calling them later to reschedule. What a lot of work! And do you think the attendees of the manager's meeting are able to focus on what she wants to discuss?

Recurring events not only help us prepare and plan but allow others to do the same. Making your staff aware that you are not available Wednesdays from three to five p.m., or letting your family know that Thursday nights you are taking a class, helps them anticipate your absence. You can take steps at work and at home to institute rituals and routines to help reduce your stress and give you comfort.

Establishing any kind of routine takes time. Without your commitment, it won't happen. Be patient, and don't overwhelm yourself trying to totally revamp your current schedule. Start with one new routine, and once that is going well, add a second and a third.

The comfort you will find in your routine will become

evident. And as you establish additional rituals, you will become more flexible with your schedule. Wow! Flexibility, reduced stress ... from concept to reality, you can do it.

Next Steps

1. Look at a weekly or monthly calendar. Enter all of your established commitments for work and home.
2. Create a short list of activities you would find beneficial as routines/rituals, such as reading e-mail at established times, meeting with colleagues, doing administrative paperwork, filing expense reports, taking care of household activities (grocery shopping, laundry, dry cleaning drop-off and pickup), preparing meals (Wednesday is pasta night, Thursday is chicken), exercising, studying, and enjoying fun time.
3. Determine the length of time you need for a particular activity and an appropriate time that will fit into your current schedule.
4. Reexamine your current commitments and see if there are ways to eliminate or simplify certain activities.
5. Block out time on your schedule for the routine activity.
6. Commit to do it.

S

Slow Down

Slow: characterized by little activity; become less tense, rest, or take one's ease

There is more to life than increasing its speed.
—Mahatma Gandhi, Indian leader

A high-powered executive for a large company was on her way home. To make her drive more productive, she typically made calls on her cell phone. When she finally pulled her SUV into her driveway, still talking, she got out of the car. Suddenly, she was knocked down by the open car door as her SUV started to roll down the driveway. As she lay there with phone in hand, the car rolled over her ankle. Fiction? Unfortunately, this is a true story. Because she was in such a hurry to get out of the car and keep talking, she didn't turn the motor off. Her productivity came to an abrupt halt!

Many years ago, there was a commercial on TV showing a family getting ready in the morning. The parents got the school-age kids in the car and then walked out the door with briefcases and coffee cups in hand. Suddenly they looked at each other, and one asked the other, "Who has Joey?" Joey, their toddler, was left behind, sitting in his high chair at the kitchen table.

A news anchor at a luncheon related a similar story in a keynote address. She was excited to attend her daughter's Girl Scout troop meeting. She left work and arrived at the meeting, noting to the meeting host that she was actually on time. She was warmly greeted by the troop leader, who asked, "Did you forget something?" The news anchor, confused at first, then realized that she had forgotten to pick up her daughter.

These are examples of Hurry Sickness. It's not a new phenomenon; in fact, the phrase Hurry Sickness originated over forty years ago when a prominent cardiologist noticed that all of his heart-disease patients had common behavior characteristics, the most apparent being that they were in a chronic rush.

It used to be that overnight mail was sent only as a last

resort; now even mundane things are sent overnight mail. E-mail isn't fast enough anymore, so we use instant messaging and text each other. A baked potato takes forty-five to sixty minutes to cook in a conventional oven. Now we can cook one in only ten minutes in a microwave, but we still find ourselves getting impatient during the last thirty seconds.

Have you hurriedly clicked the "Reply" or "Reply All" button in response to an e-mail and then realized that you made a big mistake pressing the "Send" button? Trying to call someone too fast could mean redialing if you mess up the phone number. The outcome of hurrying means the possibility of doing something again and ultimately wasting more time.

As technology is getting faster, our patience is getting shorter.

What kind of image do you send to your clients if you are always in a hurry? You could project the image that you don't have time for them or their business.

Some people are embarrassed if they are not excessively busy or in a rush like everyone else. I've had many clients exclaim in jubilation, "I didn't even have time to go to the bathroom today!" or ask me, facetiously, "Who has time to eat?" This is nothing to be proud of. There is nothing wrong with slowing down. Flaunt your ability to relax.

If you have children, what message are you sending them? Do you want them to grow up to be just like you? Perhaps you see your child rebelling against your fast-paced style by slowing down so much that you perceive him or her to be lazy.

Rushing around can become a habit—a way of life—and stress-related illness may be close at hand. Medical research cites not only physical symptoms like heart attacks, palpitations, depression, anxiety, immune disorders, and digestive ills from rushing around but an escalation in degree and intensity that leads to rudeness, short-tempered behavior, and even violence. Road rage is now more common than ever.

Hurry up and slow down!

Next Steps

1. Decide that you want to slow down.
2. Breathe. Take slow, deep breaths.
3. Do something that you enjoy that requires you to slow down.
4. Resist the temptation to respond in an instant to e-mail, voice mail, telephone calls, and text messages.
5. Leave yourself extra time to get to where you want to go.
6. Think about what you need to do or take with you ahead of time.
7. Prepare tomorrow's attire the night before.
8. Find something pleasant to do on your commute.
9. Be in the moment and enjoy it; don't think about everything else you need to be doing.
10. Laugh at the people around you who are rushing. When you really watch them, you will realize how foolish the busyness is and that life is too short to rush through.

T

Time Traps

Time trap: when you plan to get something done and get pulled away into doing something else and have difficulty getting back to what you need to do. Whatever pulls you away is a time trap!

Here we are, trapped in the amber of the moment. There is no why. —Kurt Vonnegut, American writer

There are so many time traps to cover, and it didn't seem that each time trap deserved its own chapter in *It's About Time!* So I thought I would dedicate one chapter to many time traps, give strategies for common time traps, and offer appropriate time tips in the process.

Time Trap: Not Planning

Time Tip: When you're terribly busy, planning is often the first thing to go. But planning should be your first to-do! When you are too busy and think you don't have time to plan—plan. If things are slower than usual and you think you don't need to plan—plan. Keep planning, because what you are doing is perpetuating the habit to plan. When you're busy, planning helps you focus and reduce your stress. When things are slower, you have an opportunity to plan and strategize, as well as stay in the habit of planning.

Time Trap: Meetings Without an Agenda

Time Tips:
- Have a written agenda that has a start and stop time.
- State the objective/purpose of the meeting.
- Each agenda item should have a specific purpose: information, discussion, decision-making, brainstorming, or solving a problem.
- High-priority items should be placed higher on the agenda than less-important items. If not, you run the

risk of running out of time or rushing through something that is important.

- Additional agenda items should be submitted prior to the meeting in writing (with a stated purpose).

Time Trap: Not Listening

Time Tip: This is quite obvious—listen. When someone is speaking to you, listen. If you are trying to do something else at the same time, you are bound to miss information that could be important or that you will have to ask for again. Or you'll end up having to do something over again because you weren't listening to what was asked of you.

Time Trap: E-mail

There are volumes of books and articles written about e-mail and ways to work e-mail so it doesn't work you. I've whittled down some of that information into easy to use tips.

Time Tips:
- *Subject lines* should be specific and contain dates or deadlines. Having this information in the subject line helps it stand out from other e-mails, especially when scrolling through an overflowing inbox. For example, "Board Meeting, Thursday, May 14 at 7:00 p.m."
- *Messages* should begin with essential deadlines, key information, and actions that the recipients must take. Write a clear, concise message, using bullet points to highlight relevant information as often as possible. This makes your message easier to read and makes it more likely to be read.
- *Reply* expectations should be made clear. For instance, if

you don't want or need people to "Reply All," then say it: "E-mail your response directly to me and do not Reply All." If you do not want someone to respond back at all, make that clear at the top as well. For example: "A reply is not necessary."

Time Trap: Unrealistic Time Estimates

Time Tip: If you've performed a task in the past and have that history to go by, use the information to determine how long something might take. If it's the first time you're doing something—for example, using a new software program to put together a report—you might need to be more generous with the time you block out to do the work. Multiplying the amount of time you think something will take by 1.5 or 2 will give you a realistic way to figure it out. For example, the report should take one hour, so you allow yourself either one and a half or two hours (interruption-free) to get it done.

Time Trap: Vague Deadlines

Time Tip: Not clearly communicating when you want something completed by or when you will get something done leads to ambiguity. Vague terminology doesn't convey useful information. Avoid using the following jargon. Think about it. What do these really mean?

- ASAP (as soon as possible)
- when you get a chance
- when you have the time
- later in the week
- before the end of the day
- yesterday

- right away
- soon
- at your convenience
- at your earliest convenience

When you see a sign on a storefront door that says "Be back in twenty minutes" and there is no indication when the sign was put up, the information isn't very helpful because the question becomes, twenty minutes from when?

On the other hand, many traffic lights count down the amount of time you have to cross the street. When the signal says "Walk" and you see a countdown from thirty seconds, you know how much time you have to cross.

Time Trap: Interruptions

Time Tips:
- Avoid spontaneous meetings. Instead, schedule them, even if it's within the next fifteen or thirty minutes of when you are interrupted.
- If someone pops in, explain that this isn't a good time to meet but that you want to meet them, and then schedule the time.
- Predetermine the length of the meeting and stick to it.
- Pre-establish the reason for the meeting.
- Clarify your expectations of the people who ask for meetings. Let them know that they need to come prepared with all pertinent information, questions, notes, and documents.
- Focus on the subject. If a new subject comes up, schedule another meeting.
- Keep distractions to a minimum. If necessary, meet in

a private office or conference room. Avoid answering or looking at your smartphone, e-mails, and texts.

- Close doors to avoid additional interruptions (if there are doors that can be closed).
- Keep track of time. Look at your watch before you begin and occasionally glance down at it. Don't be rude, be aware.
- Stand during a meeting to quicken the pace.
- Walk out of your space as you talk.
- Keep the discussion focused and concise, and then wrap it up.
- Be available when you say you're going to be available.
- Schedule appointments to meet with coworkers, even if they are short, ten-minute meetings.
- Give better and clearer instructions when you delegate work to others.
- Ask questions when someone is delegating work to you. Make sure you understand their expectations.

Time Trap: Interrupting Others

It's easy to see how others interrupting you can be a time trap, but have you thought about the fact that when you interrupt others, you may be causing not only a time trap for them but also a time trap for yourself? Looking at ways to avoid being the interrupter can put you in a much better light with those around you.

Time Tip: Think first before going to someone to get the information you need. Ask yourself the following questions:
- Can I figure it out on my own? Are there places to get the information without barging in on someone else? Could

I find answers I need in reference material, the Internet, the Intranet, social networks, or manuals?

- Could sending an e-mail be a time trap waiting to happen for *me*? Will I have to wait for a response, and if so, will that hold up *my* progress? Am I just being lazy?
- Do I rationalize the interruption because I'm working on a tight timeline?
- What message am I sending to my coworkers each time I interrupt them? What will I learn by doing it on my own?
- Do I need to be better trained so that I don't have to bother someone else? And if so, to whom do I speak about getting more training?

If you are one of the guilty ones who interrupts others before exhausting alternatives, don't! If you need information from an associate, don't wait until the last minute. Plan ahead of time or schedule a meeting to discuss what you need.

Take the opportunity to become more valuable to your organization. Be resourceful. Feel the sense of accomplishment that comes with doing things on your own. Respect the time of those around you.

Time Trap: Open-Door Policy

An open-door policy is great, but the reality is that many people act as if they are entitled to walk into someone's office or cubicle, willy nilly, and have a meeting. Many companies have an open-door policy but, unfortunately, no guidelines or protocol to go with it.

Time Tips:
- Find out if your company has an open-door policy.

- Discuss the open-door policy openly to ensure that it's working. Does it facilitate or impede productivity?
- Work with your team or department to put together some interruption protocols on which everyone can agree. For example, establish a company-, team-, or department-wide non-interruptible "quiet hour."
- Create an organizational chart detailing the appropriate go-to person or people for specific needs.
- Have an understanding that if workers close their door or put a sign on their cubicle stating that they are working on a deadline, it should be respected and should not be regarded as indication that someone isn't a team player.
- Everyone needs to stick to the decision regarding open-door etiquette.
- Communicate to coworkers when you need to have uninterrupted time as well as when you will be available to talk to them. Use e-mail or put a sign outside your cubicle or on your door.
- Don't use negative messages like "Do Not Disturb" or "Busy, Stay Out!"

Time Trap: Self-Sabotage and Procrastination

Self-sabotage means knowingly putting something off until later that we will regret or forget … later. Procrastination is one of the most common ways we sabotage ourselves. At some time or another, we all follow Scarlett O'Hara's credo from *Gone With the Wind*: "Tomorrow is another day." But at what cost? Here are a few common excuses for procrastination:

- It's such a big project.
- I may not succeed.
- I don't like doing it.

- I don't want to do it.
- I work better under pressure.

Time Tips:
- Think about the end results and the first step. Starting can be the most difficult part of any project.
- Break the project down into small actions and reward yourself after completing each part.
- Consider the obstacles that may get in your way. What steps can you take to overcome each obstacle? Do you have enough information? Do you need to talk to someone? Do you need help to get it done? What is the worst possible outcome if you are unsuccessful?
- Determine if this is your sole responsibility.
- Give yourself small incentives.
- Limit the amount of time you spend on the task. For example, work for fifteen minutes and then stop. Take a break, do something else—or, if you are making headway, continue.
- If you like tension, action, and risk-taking, look for other ways to get your adrenaline rush. Don't procrastinate to get that fix.
- What do you gain by actually doing whatever it is that you are procrastinating? Does it outweigh not doing it?
- "Planned procrastination" means deliberately putting something off or not doing it. It's a proactive way to take more control over how you manage yourself by making decisions and choices. Either decide it isn't something you need to do at all or schedule it for a better time.

Time Trap: Not Asking Questions

I never learn anything talking. I only learn things when I ask questions. —Lou Holtz, American football coach

How often, growing up, did we hear a teacher, coach, or parent say, "Do you have any questions? And remember, there are no stupid questions." You felt lulled into believing that it was okay to ask your question, only to have your classmates laugh when you did. You need to move beyond the embarrassment.

Time Tips:
- Asking questions is key to getting things done without wasting time or having to do something twice. Asking questions gives us a way to make sure we understand and are on the same page with others.
- When we discussed delegating earlier in the book, I introduced you to GPS—goal, purpose, and scope. This is important information for putting together an effective way to get things done. This formula helps discern what information you have and also gives a framework to weigh what information is lacking.
- A huge time trap is not having enough information. Once you have exhausted all means available to you, ask questions. If you don't ask, you don't get answers. Without answers, you are stuck, and if you are stuck, the tendency is to put whatever it is aside, leading to incomplete tasks and missed deadlines.
- When asking a question, don't apologize for not knowing information—just ask.

Time Trap: Perfection

Perfection is overrated. There are times and places where perfection counts. When adding numbers for a budget or finalizing documents that should be without spelling and grammar errors, perfection matters. However, those documents or e-mails may be written and rewritten and reedited for content, unnecessarily wasting a lot of time.

Time Tips:
- Be honest with yourself as you evaluate whether something truly needs to be perfect or you can let it go and it's good enough. This doesn't mean you can "mail it in" or do something that's just okay; it's recognizing when something really *is* okay. It's your realization that something is taking way too long, and you need to either get help or let it go.
- Ask yourself if your pursuit of perfection might really be procrastination. I had a client proclaim that she was a perfectionist. She needed to work on a project, but she was waiting for the "right time" to begin it. As we talked more about this, I revealed to her that she wasn't a perfectionist but a procrastinator. Are you really striving for the perfect time to do something or start a project, or are you merely justifying putting it off?
- Perfection is overrated and an energy drain. A perfectionist must be able to accept his or her own imperfections and the imperfections of others as well.

Next Steps

1. Identify your time traps that pull you into doing something that you shouldn't be doing and make it difficult getting back to what you need to do.

2. If you have several, choose one that has the greatest consequences on your productivity.
3. Determine one strategy that will reduce your temptation to get caught in your time trap.
4. Anticipate that time trap and nip it in the bud.

U

Unofficial Office Hours

Unofficial office hours: informal time during which a professional person or office conducts regular business

Office hours are from twelve to one, with an hour off for lunch. —George S. Kaufman, American playwright

Unofficial office hours are the ones that *you* designate, each and every day, whether at work or at home, as the best times for an interrupter to usurp some of your attention.

How often are you in the middle of a project when someone interrupts your focus and concentration? That someone could be a coworker, your manager, or your child if you have a home office. What typically happens when a coworker comes to you or calls you needing "just a few minutes" of your time?

You can say, "Sure, come on in," or you can say, "This isn't a good time, let's schedule time." The former may not be in the best interest of completing the work you need to do, or of having a conversation either—you may ask the person to sit and talk but be distracted because there are other things you need to be doing. The latter option, under most circumstances, is a much better solution. It allows you to work out a more appropriate time to reconnect. However, it can take time to figure out a mutually good time to get back together. You may have to do it through e-mail, which tends to involve a lot of back and forth.

That's why having predetermined best hours to meet or talk will save you time and angst when it comes to turning people away. These are your unofficial office hours. In some work environments, managers post their office hours. That way, employees know their manager's availability. It's time that is set aside for the sole purpose of having the door open for anyone to drop in to talk or discuss a specific matter. There are other business environments that would frown upon managers, supervisors, or contributors posting or announcing office hours.

These office hours are unofficial, and you may be the only one who knows that you have them.

The benefits of having unofficial office hours instead of official office hours include having more flexibility because you are determining, on a daily basis, when you would like to meet with folks. If you have posted hours, then you are, or at least should be, locked into those hours. You are determining, in this instance, how you want to control your schedule—what works for you. This also includes how much time you give for those unofficial office hours.

By having unofficial office hours, you are also letting your associates know that you are available in a variety of ways—by phone, by e-mail, or in person. In addition, by reserving time, even unofficially, you are giving yourself time to work. This can be a great time to read and catch up on administrative stuff. It's not the time to work on something that is difficult or requires a lot of thought.

Not knowing if someone will take advantage of your unofficial office hours makes it challenging to plan too much in that timeframe. The more you can actually schedule someone for your unofficial office hours, the better you will be able to figure out what you can do during your free time when visitors are not there. You may not have any "unofficial" meetings on a given day. And just because it's an unofficial office hour doesn't mean that it needs to be an hour at all: fifteen or twenty minutes of unscheduled, unofficial time can work. You are the one who decides.

Next Steps

1. Each day, look at your schedule and determine when you can have a block of time—small or large (fifteen minutes

to one hour)—where you can meet with colleagues when something unexpected comes up.

2. When people request time, which could be face-to-face or by phone call, for example, schedule them in during that block of time.

V

Value Your Time

**Value: to consider with respect to worth,
excellence, usefulness, or importance
(as, in this case, your time)**

*Time is the coin of your life. It is the only coin you
have, and only you can determine how it will be
spent. Be careful lest you let other people spend
it for you. —Carl Sandburg, American poet*

How many people do we know who guard their time? They don't overcommit themselves. These are the people we think twice about calling, interrupting, or asking for help with something because we know how busy they are or how they protect their time.

On one hand, what they're doing may frustrate those of us who need someone to make a commitment to a project or committee because we know they will, in all likelihood, say no. Yet, on the other hand, we wish we could be more like them and have others be more respectful of our time. I believe that when we feel other people take advantage of our generosity of time, we should own our responsibility in allowing people to do this. If we don't respect our time, why should anyone else?

My client Dave, a manager at a large paper company, was susceptible to interruptions. Dave's door was always open to anyone. If an employee needed help, Dave was there, always, to assist. He would drop whatever he was working on and focus on others' needs. Oftentimes, Dave left his office and would go to a coworker's office or cubicle to work on that person's project, not returning to his office until much later in the day. It was equally common to find Dave in his office working late, while the person who had requested his help had gone home.

As Dave and I worked together on a variety of time issues, this one seemed to bother him most. Here's what Dave did: he stopped letting interruptions or new requests waylay his work. Dave took a very methodical approach to handling the interruptions.

If Dave was in the middle of a project and decided the request warranted him putting aside his project to help the interrupter, he created another block of time to work on *his* project. His planner made all the difference, because when someone would come in, he would say, "I blocked out this period of time to do a project, but I can talk to you or work on your project later today." Just knowing Dave had scheduled that work into his day seemed to be okay with his coworkers, as long as Dave consistently followed through.

Dave began to see changes in his coworkers' attitude toward interrupting him. He noticed that as he started valuing his own time, others respected it more as well. He realized he was not relinquishing control over his day to others. He talked to people, knowing his own schedule and priorities, and set expectations in a collaborative way. He continued to get his work done, on his time and terms, and continued to be seen as a team player.

Lois, a manager in a large accounting firm, enjoyed it when coworkers would come into her office, sit down, and talk. She recalled, "I had one associate who would come in at four p.m. every day and sit down to chat." Then Lois had her first child. "I have to leave usually at five p.m., so I have to get a certain amount of stuff done. I have my head down a lot more, and I need to be more in control of my own time now. I've had to keep my priorities straight. I close my door, but people come right in. However, as soon as I show people that I value my time by letting them know it's not a good time to talk or meet and that we need to schedule time, they begin to also value my time."

We can all identify people we truly believe are too busy or have way too much going on, to the extent that we are reluctant to call or even ask them to do something with us. How can you begin to value your own time more? How can you get others to respect and value your time? Until you realize that what you are doing is important, you will have difficulty valuing your time. As M. Scott Peck, the author of *The Road Less Traveled,* writes, "If we feel ourselves valuable, then we will feel our time to be valuable, and if we feel our time to be valuable, then we will want to use it well."

In addition, you must respect and value other people's time. When you need someone's time, it's important to make sure that it's a good time for him or her; acknowledge that you realize that the person is busy. Do yourself a favor and do not negate that acknowledgement by saying, "But I only need a minute of your time." That *but* negates all that you said. Instead, ask your coworker to identify a time that *would* work.

As you value your time and value and respect other peoples' time, you will see a positive change in how you and other people value your time.

Next Steps

1. Identify the people who don't seem to value your time.
2. Work on what you will say the next time a situation arises where you can see that your time is not being valued.
3. Know from your personal planning what your priorities are and what you need to get done.
4. Set realistic expectations when someone interrupts or needs something from you.
5. Be clear and confident when you communicate with others that they need to schedule time with you or it isn't a good time.

W

Waiting

**Waiting: a period of waiting;
pause, interval, or delay**

*It is strange that the years teach us patience; that
the shorter our time, the greater our capacity
for waiting.—Elizabeth Taylor, actress*

There are many times when we think we are stopping, but we are actually waiting. Waiting, for many, can be a stress-builder. On the other hand, waiting can be something to look forward to and positively anticipate.

I was speaking at an out-of-town conference during the summer a few years ago and would arrive home too late for my son's afternoon camp pickup. When describing Jonathan's pickup routine to my husband, I told him that he should be at camp no later than 4:00 p.m. He was there at 3:50 and waited in the long car line for at least twenty minutes before he made his way to the pickup area where Jonathan was brought to the car.

Stu thought it would be helpful for me to know that when he was leaving the camp at 4:10 p.m., there was no line at all. He explained that if I got to camp around 4:10 to pick Jonathan up, I wouldn't have to wait in line.

He was absolutely correct, and I knew it. But I had made a conscious decision to wait in line because it was a good time to turn the car off and read. I didn't realize it until then, and had not shared it with Stu, but I was completely aware of my decision and very happy about it.

How much time do you spend waiting? We can spend our time on hold for customer service, waiting for a friend or a business associate we're meeting, and sitting in traffic. Waiting can make some people impatient, aggravated, or just plain grumpy. As our level of patience has decreased, our need for instant gratification has grown.

Instead of dreading wait time, however, look for ways to ease the waiting. The strategy, as simple as it may seem, is to be aware of those times when you are most likely going to wait and prepare for and look forward to them. Arrange your schedule so that you have the opportunity to wait. Decide when you want to wait and have some quiet time to do nothing, or take a book, favorite CDs, MP3 player, bills to pay, e-mails to respond to, or a list of calls you've been wanting to make.

Now don't interpret this to mean that you'll be more productive by waiting until the last minute to leave so you'll get more done. Quite the contrary—having time for yourself, and *deciding* to have time for yourself, puts you more in control of your day. When you're in control, you are less stressed, and it snowballs into positive energy. You can't eliminate waiting; it's going to happen. Decide to wait, and waiting may become one of the simpler pleasures you can enjoy. Your attitude toward waiting will make a difference.

A positive attitude causes a chain reaction of positive thoughts, events, and outcomes. It is a catalyst, a spark that creates extraordinary results.—Anonymous

Next Steps

1. Think about the most annoying time you've had to wait.
2. In hindsight, what could you have done to enhance the waiting time—a book you were in the middle of reading, the audio book you've been trying to finish, one of the magazines that never get read?
3. Identify potential waiting times.
4. Take a step back and choose what you can and will do to enjoy waiting.

X

X Marks the Spot

X marks the spot: indicating the exact location

Your journey from chaos to calm begins with an X; it is your X that marks your spot ... the place you wish to begin.—Mitzi Weinman

When I began writing *It's About Time!*—using the alphabet to illustrate techniques and tips to turn chaos into calm—I realized I would have a daunting task when I came to the letter X. What organizing concept could I share with you that begins with the letter X? As I looked through several dictionaries, I came up empty.

So, as we get closer to the end of the alphabet and the end of this book, and we arrive at the letter X, I ask for a little poetic license as we focus on X with "X Marks the Spot." When we hear that phrase, we tend to think of the place where treasure is buried on a treasure map. It's a target that has been marked out.

Now is the time for you to begin to pick your own target. Where do you begin turning chaos into calm? This book offers you a variety of strategies. As with so many things today, we tend to want to transform ourselves in a nanosecond into something or someone better. We commonly refer to this as the "clicker mentality," a need for instant gratification. Many self-improvement shows take place in a thirty- or sixty-minute time slot (with commercials) and, *voilà!*, someone's life is turned around, usually for the better.

The reality is that any significant and meaningful changes we make to better ourselves take commitment and time. That is why this chapter, "X Marks the Spot," can help you get on track to make adjustments to what you are currently doing and get you where you want to be through focused and deliberate action.

Choose one thing: one closet to clean out, one shelf to organize. Decide to go to bed fifteen minutes earlier each night and get more sleep. Block out one thirty-minute period in your calendar for a specific task.

Put your X somewhere and start with one thing that will make a difference in how you approach each day. This is your time to decide. No need to listen to anyone but yourself. Has something happened recently to cause you to think, *I wish I was better organized*, or ask yourself, *Why am I always running around, doing things at the last minute?*

What do you want to do differently so that you begin turning your chaos or minor chaos into calm? Make your mark. Draw that X.

Next Steps

1. Mark your X.
2. Determine your first next step.
3. Determine when you will take the first step and put it in the task list on your planner or calendar.
4. Follow the mantra "Do it!"

Y

Yes

Yes: used to express acknowledgment, affirmation, consent, agreement, or approval or to answer when one is addressed

You may never know what results come of your actions, but if you do nothing, there will be no result.—Mahatma Gandhi, Indian leader

In an earlier chapter, the ability to say no was the topic. And now we are at Y, and I feel it's appropriate to look at the importance and effectiveness of *yes*. That's a word that can open up a world of possibilities and opportunities. Saying yes with conviction and enthusiasm is infectious to us and those around us.

Have you ever been asked to do something by someone who is just so upbeat and positive that you can't help but want to be part of whatever he or she is involved in? And then, when you say yes, you are excited and enthusiastic about participating? That individual is a leader who has conviction, and his or her conviction is contagious to others. When you say yes, you want to make sure that your yes aligns with your goals and priorities and that you truly believe and want to say yes. When you are wishy-washy or start second-guessing your yes, you could be facing an uphill battle. Listen to your inner voice, and pay attention to your gut!

When a client, Larry, was job-searching and in desperate need of finding work, he was offered a position with a large firm. He called me, and we talked about his choice of taking it, which would mean a steady income after months of unemployment. He seemed pretty convinced by his practical and logical side that this was the way to go.

However, as we talked more, I could hear the less-than-enthusiastic tone in his voice that led me to suggest that he pass on this opportunity. It was a risk to say no. However, there was something negative emanating from him that made it evident to me, and then to him, that this was not the job for him.

A few weeks later, Larry called about another job offer. This time, his voice was filled with energy and excitement. He had no doubts or fears about this position. This was *it*!

Several years have passed since Larry took that job. He has become the president of the firm, and he loves the work that he is doing.

A couple of years after I started TimeFinder, the managing partner of a large accounting firm in Boston hired me as his coach to help him with time issues. Because he found the coaching helpful and could see the progress he was making, Sam asked me if I could do a workshop for the managers at the firm.

The work I was doing at that time was exclusively coaching— working one-on-one with clients and helping them with time, clutter, and in general, organization. The thought of doing workshops had never entered my mind. But now, the managing partner of this large accounting firm was asking me to do something that I had never done before. I probably should have answered, "No, I just do coaching," but something inside, who knows what it was, made me answer quite differently.

I said, "Yes, I can do that!" And that is just what I did. I developed a workshop for the managers, delivered it, and went on to develop more and more workshops and lunch programs, which led to speaking engagements. Who knows what would have happened if I had said no? But I know the positive results of what happened because I said yes. This was a turning point for TimeFinder and me.

What is important when saying yes is being really clear with yourself as to why you are saying yes. What is your motivation behind the yes? If you are not sure and you are waffling, you are probably not committed to whatever it is you just agreed to do. Saying yes to be nice is not a good enough reason to say yes.

Here are some questions that my clients use to determine their motivation. Once you figure that out, it may make it easier to make a decision.

- Is it something that you are doing from your heart? Are you passionate about it?
- Will a "yes" potentially enhance your business/career?
- Is it out of obligation?

Remember, we are talking about making the choice to say yes, not a situation where you are required to do something as part of your job and there is no choice involved. I'm describing a situation that allows you to opt out. This is why, when you are making a decision, you need to understand your motivation. What's in it for you? Or what's in it for someone else? Making the decision is based on both a commitment to yourself and to someone else.

The TimeFinder Honesty and Reality Check, as described in an earlier chapter, can provide guidance in this situation. You must be honest with yourself before you say yes to something. A yes to all four of the following questions is required; there is no room for a "sorta" or "maybe" or "I'm not quite sure, but I think so."

1. Do I really want to make it happen?
2. Am I being realistic?

3. If necessary, am I willing to work at it over a period of time?

4. Am I willing to reevaluate and make adjustments to my current activities?

Think about a time when you needed to make a decision. Apply the reality test, even now, in hindsight. Would your decision have been different if you'd asked yourself these questions? Think about something that you're contemplating now. Try using the reality check, and be honest with yourself.

Being committed to yes and understanding why you are saying yes will help clarify your thinking before making a decision.

Next Steps

1. Incorporate TimeFinder's Honesty and Reality Check into your decision-making.
2. Understand your yes motivation.
3. Commit to your yes!

Z

ZZZ's

ZZZ's: slang for sleep—to take the rest afforded by a suspension of voluntary bodily functions and the natural suspension, complete or partial, of consciousness; cease being awake.

Have courage for the great sorrows of life and patience for the small ones; and when you have laboriously accomplished your daily task, go to sleep in peace.—Victor Hugo, French writer

The last chapter of *It's About Time!* is all about catching some zzz's—that is, the importance of sleep as part of a healthy lifestyle and productivity. This is an area that many of us tend to scrimp on, not getting the much-needed sleep that we require. Too often I've heard a client boast that he or she can survive on four hours of sleep a night. I always ask, "What's the point? You really can't be as effective as you may think you are."

In an article for the *Harvard Business Review* entitled "Sleep Deprivation's True Workplace Costs," Patrick J. Skerrett wrote about a study conducted by Mark Rosekind, a member of the National Transportation Safety Board and founder of Alertness Solutions, a company that "translates the science of fatigue into powerful, impactful solutions that improve safety and performance," and Debra Lerner, MS, PhD, director of the program in health, work, and productivity at the Institute for Clinical Research and Health Policy Studies. The study showed that employees don't get enough sleep and that sleep deficiency costs employers millions of dollars each year because productivity goes down. Skerrett also reported that

> lost productivity due to poor sleep cost $3,156 per employee with insomnia, and averaged about $2,500 for those with less severe sleep problems. Across four companies, sleep-related reduction in productivity cost $54 million a year. This doesn't include the cost of absenteeism—those with insomnia missed work an extra five days a year compared to good sleepers.

I interviewed Dr. Lawrence J. Epstein, instructor in medicine at Harvard Medical School, director of the Sleep Clinic, and program director of the Sleep Medicine Fellowship Program at Brigham and Women's Hospital. He says that there is an ideal number of hours a person should sleep. It varies from person to person, but in most people it ranges from 7.5 to 8.5 hours a night. Some individuals may need more. He strongly suggests the importance of figuring out your sleep needs.

How do you do that? According to Dr. Epstein, take a period of time (vacation) and go to bed for as long as you need. By the end of vacation, you should wake up around the same time each day, refreshed. That's the amount of time you need. Once you learn the amount of sleep you require, carve it out and protect it. Being consistent with the amount of sleep you get every night improves health and functioning, and makes you a more productive worker.

During the weekends, we tend to change our sleeping habits and stay up later and sleep later. This makes us more tired on Monday, creating what is known as "Monday morning fatigue."

Chronic or Partial Sleep Deprivation

When we continue to lose hours of sleep over a period of time, we build up a sleep debt, and our performance declines. According to Dr. Epstein, "After two weeks of sleeping four to six hours a night, performance is as bad as if we were awake for more than forty-eight hours." In addition, those who say they don't notice any difference in their productivity when they have chronic partial sleep deprivation are in no position to make judgments in this area. People who are sleep-deprived are poor at deciding how much they are impaired. They can't tell. Their judgment is off.

Additionally, sleep deprivation contributes to cardio problems, hypertension, obesity, diabetes, and a shortened life span. Too much sleep and too little sleep both shorten one's life.

Naps

In 2010, sleep researcher James B. Maas delivered a speech at the UP Experience and suggested the "Power Nap" to anyone who can't get adequate sleep. Dr. Maas explained to his audience that he invented the phrase in 1974. He defined the power nap as, "something that doesn't last more than ten to fifteen minutes, just enough to get you through the rest of the day but not so much as to put you in delta or deep sleep and make you groggy when you get up. And not so much as to cause you nocturnal insomnia."

In an article, entitled "Power Napping for Increased Productivity," for Lifescript, a website dedicated to women's health, Rose Alexander wrote, "Boston University Professor Dr. William Anthony and Camille Anthony, co-presidents of The Napping Company, claim that scientific evidence shows that napping improves mood and performance. Increased productivity on the job or at home may just be the tip of the iceberg in terms of benefits gleaned from power napping."

Dr. Epstein thinks that naps, when you're sleepy, can refresh and wake you up. He says that if they are needed, however, it's a sign that you are not getting enough sleep. Sleeping during the day can make it difficult to sleep at night. He warns that naps can make later sleeping more difficult, but they can make you feel less sleepy after the nap. He suggests taking a nap when you need to be alert to do something. For example, when you are going to be driving and you are sleepy, take a thirty- to forty-five-minute nap.

Because of our circadian rhythm (internal clock), we sleep when it's dark and are awake during the light. We are physiologically programmed to be awake at certain times. The siesta works when night sleep is shorter, and a nap or siesta makes up for the lack of night sleep.

Our bodies require a certain amount of sleep over twenty-four hours. Prime sleep time is the middle of the night and mid-afternoon. We need to balance our sleep to get the required number of hours our bodies need. It can be broken up into blocks of time—a block at night and the balance of sleep in the daytime.

Sleep inertia is the time it takes to get from sleep to full alertness; the longer the nap, the deeper the stage of sleep, the longer the period to full alertness. To become alert, a shorter nap is best. Keep in mind the following "Power Nap Action List":

- Bring a mat to work.
- If you have an office, turn out the lights and close the door.
- If you work in a cubicle, find some privacy. If necessary, use your car.

- Talk to an appropriate person at work to discuss the benefits of napping.
- Only nap fifteen to twenty minutes; any longer will negate the purpose of the power nap by making you sluggish and groggy.
- Take a nap only if you are tired.

Sleep improves performance, learning, and memory. When we "sleep on it," we are rethinking information. We learn better if we sleep well. When we get a good night's sleep, we retain information; it's the time to turn off and relax. Don't undervalue the importance of sleep.

Next Steps

1. Realize the importance of sleep and its impact on productivity and general health.
2. Make enough time for sleep.
3. Have a regular routine for sleeping (number of hours, when you go to bed and wake up).
4. Avoid things that disrupt sleep, such as alcohol and caffeine.
5. Living an overall healthy lifestyle improves sleep.
6. If problems with sleep occur, see a doctor.

Conclusion

Wow! Just writing the word *conclusion* is amazing! This is a project many years in the making. But the reality is, there is no conclusion. Transforming your chaos into calm is a process, and it takes commitment over time to get to where you want to be. It's a one-step-at-a-time progression. The commitment is from *you* to *you* alone.

Several years ago, after giving birth to my son, Jonathan, I had put on some weight. I had always been quite thin—some would even say too thin. Having extra weight was so unnatural to me. I kept telling myself that I wanted to lose the weight, I really wanted to lose the weight.

I decided that I would begin to exercise: wake up half an hour early every morning, go upstairs to our finished attic, put on music, and dance (dancing is one of my passions, having started out in college as a dance major). I even bought pointe shoes as a way to really get back in shape.

For the first few days, when the alarm went off, I got up and trudged up the stairs, put the music on, and began to dance. But after four or five days, I realized that although I wanted to lose weight, I also wanted to sleep a little longer, and I *really* didn't want to get up. So I stopped and just went on about my daily life.

Many months went by, and one of my clients suggested I get a recumbent bike. It's a stationary bike that has a back to it. This seemed perfect, because I had a bad back. I could put my music in my Walkman and bike.

The recumbent bike was great, and because I didn't like getting up early in the morning to exercise, I decided that I would pick a time that worked best for me. That made a difference. However, even doing the recumbent bike sporadically, my weight just kept going up. Apparently, I wasn't *really* ready to do anything about it.

And then it happened. Within two weeks, three people asked me when I was due. *Yikes!* That was hurtful and caused me much pain and sadness. What did I look like that three people in a short span of time thought I was pregnant?

That was it! That was the motivation I needed. I took out my journal (I don't usually journal unless I need to vent privately) and wrote:

February 9, 2004—I weigh 139 pounds. I don't know what my resistance was to get on the scale but I finally did it this morning. It wasn't as bad as I thought it would be but it is not good. Three people within two weeks have asked me if I am expecting. This makes me angry and sad!

I am changing my eating. I started this morning. I want to be vibrant and sexy and have a body that not only Stu will be proud of but I will be as well. I want Jonathan to think he has a fabulous mom who is in great shape and pretty.

He'll tell me I'm pretty (he's so sweet), but I want more & I'm going to get it.

I am so grateful to have my health. Jonathan, Stu, Ralph & Edna are also healthy! We're building a beautiful house and life is really terrific. Now I need to get out of my way and get the weight off and firm up my tummy.

I took charge, I took control, and I decided, first and foremost in my head and heart, that I was going to do this. By October 2004, I had lost thirty-two pounds!

The point of the story is that the commitment came from my head and my heart first. Your commitment to change or even tweak or make minor adjustments to how you approach your day must be something that you are committed to, head and heart.

The Honesty and Reality Check is mentioned several times in *It's About Time!* because it's that important. It's an absolute must for all who read this book. As a reminder, you must answer *yes* to the following questions:

1. Do I really want to make it happen?
2. Am I being realistic?
3. If necessary, am I willing to work at it over a period of time?
4. Am I willing to reevaluate and make adjustments to my current activities?

There is a Broadway show tune (for me there is always a Broadway show tune) from *The Roar of the Greasepaint - The Smell of the Crowd*, words and lyrics by Anthony Newley and Leslie Bricusse, that sums it up: "Nothing Can Stop Me Now!" The positive message is that you can find your success today. Don't let your yesterdays get in your way. Your yesterdays are filled with lessons to learn but shouldn't stop you from moving forward. It's about making a promise and commitment to yourself. Nothing can stop you now except *you*! You can do what you set your mind to, and by taking small steps, you will ensure your success at Transforming Chaos into Calm.

Need a little more time with Mitzi? This can be arranged. Mitzi Weinman offers a variety of programs and topics as a speaker, trainer, and coach for companies, groups, and associations of all sizes. In addition, Mitzi is available for personal and group coaching in person and through a number of technological opportunities.

To learn more about the possibilities, contact Mitzi by e-mail at Mitzi@TimeFinder.net. You can also visit her website at TimeFinder.net and find her blog, helpful tips, and other resources.

Contact Mitzi Weinman
TimeFinder
www.TimeFinder.net
Mitzi@TimeFinder.net
781-444-3220

Works Cited

Definitions at the beginning of each chapter originate from www.Dictionary.com. Quotations at the beginning of each chapter and throughout the manuscript were found on the following sites: www.BrainyQuote.com, www. ThinkExist.com, www.izquotes.com, www.Quotes.net, www.inspirationalstories.com, www.QuotationsPage.com, and www.successnet.org/library2.htm. The following books, articles, speech and CD were also referenced.

Alexander, Rose. "Power Napping for Increased Productivity." Lifescript. www.lifescript.com. June 28, 2007.

Covey, Stephen. *First Things First*. New York: Free Press, 2003.

Epstein, Lawrence. Interview by Mitzi Weinman. October 22, 2012.

Hill, Napoleon. *Think and Grow Rich*. Hollywood: Wilshire Book Company, 1966.

Loehr, Jim, and Tony Schwartz. *The Power of Full Engagement*. New York: Free Press, 2003.

Maas, James. Dr. James Maas at the UP Experience 2010. YouTube, 27:28. September 19, 2011. http://youtu.be/GxEJTNEtIKY.

Newley, Anthony, and Leslie Bricusse. *Nothing Can Stop Me Now*. The Roar of the Greasepaint - The Smell of the Crowd, CD, 1965.

Peck, Scott. *The Road Less Traveled.* New York: Simon and Schuster, 1978.

Sher, Barbara. *I Could Do Anything If I Only Knew What It Was: How to Discover What You Really Want and How to Get It.* New York: Random House, 2010.

Skerrett, Patrick J. "Sleep Deprivation's True Workplace Costs." HBR Blog Network, *Harvard Business Review.* January 12, 2011.

Vilet, Jacque. "Company Goals: Do Your Employees Have a 'Line of Sight' to Them." TLNT. www.tlnt.com. June 7, 2012.

Resources

Animoto: www.animoto.com
Daytimer: www.DayTimer.com
Google Calendar: www.google.com/calendar
Microsoft Outlook: www.microsoft.com/en-us/outlook-com/

About the Author

Mitzi Weinman was *not* born organized, in fact, she continues to work at it every day. Through her journey – and those of her clients – she has learned various life-enhancing ways to approach organization and personal productivity.

Mitzi Weinman, founder of TimeFinder, is a coach, workshop leader and professional speaker. She helps people develop good habits and techniques to reduce stress which can result from not planning, procrastinating, feeling disorganized and overwhelmed, and rushing to get things done, at work and/or at home. Since 1989, TimeFinder's programs have provided ongoing support and professional and personal development to hundreds of companies, individuals and associations. Mitzi's many clients include: New Balance, Reebok, Boston University School of Medicine, Boston Symphony Orchestra, WGBH, Lojack, Grant Thornton, Dana Farber Cancer Institute, Weston and Sampson Engineers, Pearson Education and Marriott University. Prior to founding TimeFinder, Mitzi worked as the New England Advertising Representative specializing in recruitment advertising for the Chicago Tribune; an Account Executive for Northwest Travel selling corporate travel; a Sales Administrator for Trans National Travel; and an Account Coordinator for Buyer Advertising where she also created the Traffic Department. Throughout her career, the need to stay organized, build relationships, keep promises by following through were critical to Mitzi's work as a sales administrative assistant, account coordinator, sales representative, and entrepreneur.

Mitzi's tips and techniques appear regularly in publications, on TV and radio, including Fox 25 News, Martha Stewart Living Radio, "Making a Living with Maggie," on SiriusXM Satellite Radio, Investor's Business Daily, Boston Business Journal, American Way (American Airlines in-flight magazine), Woman's Day, Marie Claire, Redbook, Bj's Journal, Mass High Tech and more. Mitzi also publishes her own E-Newsletter, *OnTime*.

Mitzi received her B.S. from the Newhouse School of Public Communications at Syracuse University and lives in Needham, MA, with her husband, son and dog.

Index